Five Skills to Learning How to Learn

Other Books by Guinevere Durham

Teaching Test-Taking Skills: Proven Techniques to Boost Your Student's Scores

Standardized Testing Skills: Strategies, Techniques, Activities To Help Raise Students' Scores, 2nd Edition

Five Skills to Learning How to Learn

From Confusion to AHA!

Guinevere Durham

ROWMAN & LITTLEFIELD
Lanham • Boulder • New York • London

Published by Rowman & Littlefield
A wholly owned subsidiary of The Rowman & Littlefield Publishing Group, Inc.
4501 Forbes Boulevard, Suite 200, Lanham, Maryland 20706
www.rowman.com

16 Carlisle Street, London W1D 3BT, United Kingdom

Copyright © 2015 by Guinevere Durham

All rights reserved. No part of this book may be reproduced in any form or by any
electronic or mechanical means, including information storage and retrieval systems,
without written permission from the publisher, except by a reviewer who may quote
passages in a review.

British Library Cataloguing in Publication Information Available

Library of Congress Cataloging-in-Publication Data available

ISBN 978-1-4758-1344-9 (cloth : alk. paper)
ISBN 978-1-4758-1345-6 (pbk. : alk. paper)
ISBN 978-1-4758-1346-3 (electronic)

Contents

I: The Groundwork: Understanding the Style of How We Learn

1   Introduction   1

II: The Nitty-Gritty: The What, the Why, and the How of the Five Skills

2   Logic: The Rationale   9

3   Critical Thinking: The Assurance   23

4   Problem Solving: The Process   35

5   Investigating: The Clues   47

6   Experimenting: The Proof   59

III: The Digging In

7   A Child's "Work" Is "Play"   69

8   Logic   75

9   Critical Thinking   81

10   Problem Solving   85

11   Investigating   89

12   Experimenting   95

IV: The Keeping Fit

13   Proactive Steps for Physical Health   101

V: Aha!

14   Summary and Conclusion   107

Breaking the Code: Definitions of Terms   109

Resources   113

About the Author   115

I

The Groundwork: Understanding the Style of How We Learn

ONE

Introduction

> Give a man a fish and you feed him for a day. Teach a man to fish and you feed him for a lifetime. —Chinese proverb

Using that same premise, teach children facts and data and prepare them for a test. Teach children *how* to learn the facts and data and prepare them for a lifetime.

Many retired educators of today, as they look back at their own education and how they were taught to teach, are amazed by the transformation of the process in the years of their lifetime. The process may be viewed as the one used before technology and the one in use in the age of technology. Since the 1980s, teachers have been advising parents that "we are educating students today for jobs that haven't even been created yet."

Today's youngsters have the world at their fingertips. With the click of a mouse or the touch of a screen, the educator's job is no longer to "teach the data"; rather it is to teach the children "how to learn the data." The term *educator* or *caregiver* in this book includes the classroom teacher, parent, coach, counselor, and any person dispensing information on "how-to" through print material, the media, or any type of technology. These educators, also fortunate to have the world at their fingertips, are more informed and better equipped to teach and mentor children.

Finding the information needed at the time is the lesser challenge. The major challenge is accessing, assessing, analyzing, and arriving at a summary of all the material found through the research that will meet the children's wants and needs at the time. This book, *Five Skills to Learning How to Learn,* has been written for the purpose of preparing children for a lifetime. The skills essential for this task are:

- Logic
- Critical thinking
- Problem solving

2 *Chapter 1*

- Investigating
- Experimenting

Before each skill is defined, described, and explained and before the practical, proven techniques, strategies, and activities are detailed, a short discussion is necessary to acquaint the educator with learning styles. This book is short on theory, long on hands-on ideas, and written in nontechnical terminology. However, these next few pages are vital.

Each side of the brain governs different functions for learning. One side will be dominant for a person, but the traits of the other side are also in evidence. A learning style does not make someone better or more intelligent, it simply makes them different. To clarify this, in very basic terms, a *learning style* is *how* we learn the information; *intelligence* is the ability of *how much* we are capable of learning.

In the late 1960s, research was begun that was to change the history of our appreciation of the human brain. This is when it was discovered that there are two parts of the brain, not just one. Simply put, the left side deals with logic, words, reasoning, and numbers. The right side deals with the whole picture, creativity, rhythm, images, imagination, color, and daydreaming.[1]

The chart below lists the basic characteristics of each style:

Table 1.1. Characteristics

Left Brain	Right Brain
Analytical: takes all the parts and arranges them in order to the finished product	Global: sees the whole picture, then deals with the parts as they are needed for the project
Sequential processing: step-by-step; makes lists, schedules, and plans	Random processing: varied order; flits from one task to another
Logical	Emotional
Plans ahead	Impulsive
Studying:	Studying:
formal setting; quiet; good lighting	comfortable, any place is fine; music/sound; frequent movement
Looks at differences	Looks at similarities
Speaks with few gestures	Gestures when speaking
Verbal: language, numbers	Visual: creative; music/art/dance

Do you recognize the learning style of your child? Parents and teachers today, with the advantage of knowing about learning styles, are better able to teach children how to learn for a lifetime. Family relations are also improved when a parent understands that learning style plays a role in the way children act and react as they do. The children are not being disrespectful; they are acting in sync with their learning style.

Introduction 3

An example of how the two styles work independently of and in collaboration with each other is this story about the vacation of a married couple. He was a strong right-brained person and she was equally strong left-brained. After several frustrating sessions in planning their trip, they came to a compromise.

She planned the first week and he planned the second. Her week was planned almost to the minute. They knew the exact route to drive, where to eat, and which sights to visit, and they had reservations every night for a motel. The second week was the direct opposite, for he planned nothing. His idea of a terrific vacation was to get in the car and drive and see where they ended up. They ate when they were hungry and in a restaurant that "looked good." They veered off the beaten path if they spotted a sign advertising an interesting attraction. They slept in whatever motel was available in their location. They both enjoyed themselves more than they had anticipated and also learned how to work more successfully with each other's style.

Other features also enter into the equation of how one learns. There are three approaches that, added to the left brain/right brain characteristics, dictate how a person learns and responds to life. These are called modalities.

Researchers have concluded that a classroom is composed of approximately:

- 25 to 30 percent visual learners
- 25 to 30 percent auditory learners
- 15 percent tactile/kinesthetic learners
- 25 to 30 percent mixed modalities[2]

1. Visual learner (learn by seeing): This person prefers reading print material; using the Internet; watching a presentation with Power-Point, graphics and charts; and watching plays or sports events. Visuals are needed along with the lecture for the learner to understand and remember the concept.
2. Auditory learner (learns by hearing): This person best learns by listening to a speech; listening to lectures, tapes, or television (doesn't need to watch); or in conversations. Reading information in a textbook, newspaper, or magazine or on the Internet is very tedious and an unproductive task for this person. For comprehension, the material needs to be read to them or they need to read it out loud.
3. Tactile/kinesthetic learner (learns by doing or touching): This person cannot sit still for very long and needs to be moving. This is the style of athletes, musicians, artists, craftsmen, dancers, actors, and any profession that requires a hands-on approach.

When working with children, identify their strengths (style of learning) and teach the skills through that style. One elementary teacher volunteered to drive her teammates across the state to a reading conference for their school system. A well-meaning friend gave the teacher directions—of course, they were given orally.

The teacher bought a map of the state (this was before "maps" on the Internet or before GPS systems for the automobile) and highlighted the route they were to travel. Then she wrote it out as a list with brief steps to follow for each change of directions. She visualized the map, remembered what she had written, and had no problem finding the conference center. After that incident, she started to carry a small notebook to record any information someone told her that she needed to remember. The handheld device now replaces that notebook.

Children have been told, as she had been, "You can do this, if you will try harder," or "Focus! Concentrate! There's no reason you cannot do this!" These comments may be very frustrating to a person who is conscientiously trying to do the task but is being unsuccessful. The reason children had difficulty learning the material was not because of intelligence, it was because the material was not presented in the children's learning style. Again, teach to the children's strengths.

A study begun in 1986–1987 validates this premise that children who have been taught *how* to learn, learn for a lifetime. It took place in the inner-city schools of Washington, DC. The report was written by Rebecca A. Marcon, a developmental psychologist and college professor at the University of North Florida, Jacksonville.[3]

The concerns that prompted the study were the unacceptably high first-grade retention rate and the difficult transition for students from third to fourth grade. A contributing factor in the difficult transition is the format of the school curriculum. In first through third grades the students *learn to read*. At the fourth-grade level the format changes to *reading to learn*.

The study began with three preschool groups and followed them through fourth grade. The format of the first group was *child-initiated*, that is, children selected the focus of their learning. The next group was *academic-directed*, that is, the teacher directed the instruction. The last group was *middle-of-the-road*, which was a combination of the other two. In every area, the children in this third group were the least successful.

At fourth grade it was evident that the *academic-directed* group would meet with success but were very dependent on the teacher's directions. In other words, "Tell me what to do and I will do it." However, if plan A didn't work, the children waited for the teacher to tell them the directions for plan B.

The *child-initiated* group was the most successful, for they had learned how to learn and had learned many methods in which to tackle a task. They would attempt plan A, one they had devised. If that did not work,

Introduction   5

they would simply devise plan B and work until they accomplished the task. They will not hesitate to ask for help, if needed. It does not matter what learning style is dominant for the children; they can accomplish the task their way.

This study validated what can be witnessed in elementary schools in rural areas, affluent suburbs, inner cities, and preschools. It works. There is no "right" way in which to learn.

Each of the five skills has its own chapter, containing a definition and description of the skill. Then an explanation will relate each skill to the major areas of the curriculum: language arts, math, science, and social studies. The next step is to illustrate the usefulness of the skill in areas outside the academic classroom. Each skill, in a separate chapter, is dedicated to explaining and illustrating techniques, strategies, and activities created and used by teachers in several states over a thirty-year period. These are practical, productive, and proven procedures for preparing our children for a lifetime.

There is a variety of material, so pick what works for you and your children. Don't overwhelm yourself and try to do it all. Be choosy and enjoy!

NOTES

1. Buzan, Tony. *Use Both Sides of Your Brain.* London, England: A Pluma Book (Penguin Group), 1991, page 16.
2. Rose, Colin. 1987. *Accelerated Learning* program.
3. Marcon, Rebecca A. 1986–1987. *Fourth-Grade Slump: The Cause and the Cure.* Washington, DC, preschools project.

II

The Nitty-Gritty: The What, the Why, and the How of the Five Skills

TWO

Logic: The Rationale

I never teach my pupils; I only attempt to provide the conditions in
which they can learn. — Albert Einstein

Logic is sensible, rational thought or argument (left brain) rather than
ideas that result from emotion or whim (right brain). Simply, logic is a
way of reasoning. But to be even more specific, it is a relationship between particular incidents, occasions, or happenings and the consequences of the action. Each of the five skills has several definitions from
which to choose. Select the one that will be best understood according to
the age and maturity of the children.

This skill is vital in life, at home, at school, and in the world. It can be
taught and must be initiated in the early years of the learning process.
Example: A tradition in a home at Easter was for each of the children to
place an empty Easter basket at their place setting on the kitchen table the
night before the holiday. (This tradition continued until the youngest
learned the difference between fantasy and reality.) The youngest, five
years old, placed hers on her chair rather than on the table. An older
sister moved it to the table.

"No!" the young girl replied as she moved it back to the chair. "The
Easter Bunny is little! Bunnies can't jump that high and they can only
reach the chair." Young children are capable of learning logic.

Begin the learning process with concrete activities and ideas; that is,
things the child can see or hold, something that is real or tangible. As the
child matures, so will the complexity of the task to things that are semi-
abstract, such as the category of pictures, magazines, television, and
handheld tech items. The next step is to the abstract of numbers, words,
ideas, or visions (for example, a simple addition problem: $2 + 3 = ?$).

- *Concrete:* Put two familiar items on the table. Leave a space of about
  two to three inches. Then put three like items in a row. As the

10 *Chapter 2*

children touch each item, they count aloud, thus arriving at the answer. Examples of items are blocks, pencils, paper clips, spoons, or any items found in the house. Take a picture of the display on the table and save for future use.

- *Semi-abstract:* Use the pictures taken of the displays for the concrete examples. Either show the examples from the handheld device or print them out if a paper version is preferred.
- *Abstract:* 2 + 3 = ? Write the math computation problem on paper (similar to a math workbook page). This activity may be just as effective when displayed on the computer.

During the early childhood years, logic is taught through competencies in the form of sequence, cause/effect, predicting, and summarizing. Logic is a way of life for the left-brained person. The right-brained person has a sense of logic, but it is not their primary way of learning or behaving. Handheld high-tech devices are a boon to the right-brained person. Although very unlikely to make lists and schedules on paper, these folks will avail themselves of the current technology.

SEQUENCE

Since sequence means "order of succession" or "continuity of progression," it is the logical skill with which to begin. Either style of learning will help the children reach a conclusion, but the order or progression will vary. The process, whether sequential or haphazard, will make perfect sense to the children and accomplish the assigned task.

In the Home

Consider an activity of teaching children to make a peanut butter and jelly sandwich. Actually you are teaching the children a sequential process. This is a concrete example of that process. Put your thoughts of "This is a waste of time. Everyone can do this!" aside and observe. Remember, it is the process that indicates whether the children are predominantly right-brained or left-brained. The process will vary, but the finished product will be the same. Activities similar to this one help the parent or teacher discover the key to the way in which the children learn best.

With any undertaking, adhere to the correct terminology and use a single-step command progression. The example uses the ordinal number (1st, 2nd, 3rd, etc.), but other sequential terms may be substituted (first, next, then, after that, finally). As with any lesson, gear it to the child's style and level of learning. The left-brained children will assemble all utensils and ingredients before starting. The right-brained child will get the utensils and food products as they are needed for the task. The style each child uses is the best style for that child.

- 1st: Select the dish and spreading knife (sometimes a double command is okay).
- 2nd: Find the peanut butter in the pantry.
- 3rd: Get the jelly from the refrigerator.
- 4th: Now get the bread from the bread box.
- 5th: Spread the peanut butter on one slice and then the jelly on the other slice.
- 6th: Carefully put the slices together.
- 7th (at last): Ask, "Do you want it cut or left whole?" Use your judgment as to whether children are age-appropriate for this task.

Use the same process for teaching the child to fix other simple meals (cereal and fruit for breakfast), crafts (jack-o'-lantern), and for household and personal tasks (making a bed and dressing oneself). The step-by-step process will soon become automatic, and organizing tasks will become more effective and efficient. Again, accomplishing the task with the desired results (an eatable sandwich!) is what is important; the process (sequential or out of order) is secondary.

A teacher had explained this process to one of the students' parents at a parent conference. The parent diligently taught this process to her children. A few weeks later, the parent came down with the flu. She e-mailed the teacher to thank her for the advice and stated, "It was a relief to know that my ten-year-old could make the children sandwiches for lunch." As you can see, this task has many benefits. The children also develop a sense of accomplishment and like to demonstrate their new skills for friends.

The following is a list of words to use interchangeably in teaching the skill:

- 1st, 2nd, 3rd, etc.
- Start, next, then, later, after, after that
- Begin, middle, end
- Before, after
- Finally, at last

There are times when the children may not understand the logic for the sequence of events. Many tasks are done in a specific way and are expected to be accepted as such. But children question, "Why?" Take the time to illustrate or demonstrate the rationale. Start with the concrete and teach them through their five senses. Make it a fun activity. Instead of having the child put on socks and then shoes, tell them to put on the shoes first. Then take an old pair of large-size socks (mom's or dad's) and

Chapter 2

put them on over the shoes. This will result in an interesting conversation and much laughter.

This activity, and others like it, will teach the children to use the other skills (critical thinking, problem solving, investigating, or experimenting) to answer their own question of "Why?"

Sequence may also be used to reinforce positive behavior, such as, "After you finish your homework, we will go to the mall." Or "Before we have ice cream, you will have to get out the bowls and spoons." That usually elicits an immediate response.

In the World

Learning that every task has a series of steps between the onset of the activity and its completion will also benefit the children outside the home.

- Children registering for Little League sports will accept the steps involved, including practicing, that will lead to being a proficient athlete and member of a team.
- Children beginning music or dance lessons may not relish all the hours of practice but will understand the need for them.
- Children joining a scout troop understand that a series of activities precedes the qualification for a merit badge.
- When taking a job such as mowing lawns, babysitting, or walking dogs, children understand that the task needs to be completed before the payment is received.
- Again, the finished product is the objective; the order of the steps may vary.

At School

Every skill taught has to be relevant and meaningful to children or they will see no purpose in learning it. Teachers who teach history and math have to work hard to overcome this mind-set. They are continually looking for that "teaching moment."

In a second-grade classroom in New York State, a child brought in a caterpillar that would eventually develop into a beautiful monarch butterfly. Someone took the lid off the jar (holes had been poked in the top), and the caterpillar disappeared. A few days later, the students arrived in the morning to find a beautiful light-green chrysalis attached to the edge of the countertop. The teacher had some yellow net, which she generously draped around the chrysalis and then taped the net to the counter.

The class spent part of the morning discussing what had happened and what would happen next. Finally the special day arrived. As the students walked into the classroom, they saw that the chrysalis was a transparent color. It was time. The teacher shelved the lesson plans for the day and went to plan B, which she had previously prepared for this special day. The butterfly emerged about a half hour before the close of school for the day. What an experience to watch the amazing event. The students still had their lessons:

- Reading: The teacher had prepared a story (written in second-grade language) titled "From Caterpillar to Butterfly." The sequence of events and the environment were highlighted.
- Accompanying the story was a worksheet of comprehension questions, which the children completed at their desks.
- Math: The teacher created a color-by-number full-sheet picture of the monarch butterfly outlined in black. The children colored in this worksheet, the numbers being second-grade subtraction problems. That is: If the space said "12 – 8," the child looked at the key for the number 4 (which was red) and colored it accordingly.
- Science: The students discussed insects and butterflies and the sequence of the process from caterpillar to butterfly.
- History: The teacher pulled down the hanging map of the United States, and the students located where they lived and learned where that species of butterfly lived.
- Handwriting: The teacher listed the pertinent words on the board (butterfly, caterpillar, chrysalis, emerge, environment, etc.), and the students copied them as their handwriting lesson for the day. These words are not common vocabulary for a second-grader, but they were read and learned, for they had special meaning to the children.

At the end of the day the students did what had to be done. First they gave the butterfly some sugar water on a saucer for strength, and then they took it outside to release it into its own environment. There were many "Good-bye, butterflys" and some tears. There could not have been a more meaningful and relevant activity. What a day!

CAUSE AND EFFECT

Cause: The reason the event happened
Effect: The results of what happened
Example:

1. Cause: The student completed and turned in all assignments.
2. Effect: The student made the honor roll.
3. Cause: The student ran on the playground without looking to see if someone was swinging.
4. Effect: The student was hit by the swing.
5. Cause: The driver of the car was speeding.

14 *Chapter 2*

6. Effect: The driver was stopped by a policeman and given a speeding ticket.

This is, by far, the most important and significant skill both to teach and to learn. Whatever we do will result in some sort of effect or consequences. Some will be positive and some will be negative, but we grow and develop from both types of experiences. The tendency is to "act, and then react." Learning this skill changes the mind-set to "appraise, and then act." With guidance and practice, children with either learning style can improve their judgment in this area.

By adjusting the cause, the effect may be more to your liking. For instance, because of congested traffic, the driver of the car was going to be late for an appointment. Rather than speed (and probably experience some stress), the driver simply calls ahead, explains the circumstances, and drives within the speed limit. Thus, no ticket. Remember the student who was hit by the swing? After being hit once by a swing, the student learned to be more cautious. Before running (the cause), the student looks over the area and decides where it is the safest to run. Fun is had and no one gets hurt (the effect).

When the effect of an activity turns out differently than expected and in a negative way, there is the tendency to play the blame game. One aspect of the cause/effect process is that the children must also be aware that they are responsible for their own behavior. That is, they suffer the consequences (effect) of their performance or lack of performance (cause). This is one of life's most difficult lessons.

Example: The finalists of the fifth- and sixth-grade spelling bees were in a competition for the one student who would represent the school in the county spelling bee. The twelve contestants were sitting on the stage, and the audience was their classmates. The first two rounds went well. Then on the third round a fifth-grade boy missed his word. One of the other contestants, a sixth-grade boy, grinned and applauded. The judges did not stop the behavior, for they felt the sixth-grader needed to learn the lesson from his peers.

The inappropriate behavior continued until it was down to the final three. The sixth-grade boy's word was "balloon" and he said "b-a-l-o-o-n." His smug smile quickly disappeared as the judges raised their hands to signify a wrong spelling and the audience erupted into applause and cheers.

As the class was walking back to the classroom after the competition was over, the students were chanting "B! A! L! L! O! O! N!" The classroom teacher pretended not to hear what was going on. This lesson was long in coming for this student. But he learned it well. He had quite an attitude adjustment, which was responsible for his becoming an honor student as well as a leader the next year in junior high school.

Logic: The Rationale

All situations do not have such a happy ending. This skill must be taught, modeled, explained, coached, mentored, spelled out, and instilled in the child. A principal of an elementary school in a rural school district in which 90 percent of the students were bused to school related this story. A fourth-grade boy was walking up and down the aisle as the bus was moving. He was told by the driver to sit in his assigned seat. He did not. The bus driver pulled over and said she could not safely continue to drive until he was seated. He went to the front of the bus, argued with her, and then hit her. A few older boys (high-schoolers also rode the same bus) subdued him, and the driver continued on to school.

The boy was suspended from the bus for two weeks. His mom came in to talk to the principal. She was in tears as she stated that his father was upset and that the boy should be reassigned back on the bus.

It was common knowledge (visible bruises and a broken arm) that the father physically abused the mother. The boy felt it was acceptable behavior to hit a female. The principal told the mom that she would be very happy to talk to the dad. Needless to say, the dad never came for a conference. The incident did not change the boy's behavior and thought process, but it did modify it at school and on the bus. This was not an isolated incident. There were other documented incidents in that state of similar altercations, in grade levels four through high school.

Dealing with the child after a negative effect is an important part of the whole lesson. After a first offense (sassing the teacher, taunting another student, being a bully, refusing to do class work or participate in classroom activities), a conference with the parent(s) is usually requested. Those in attendance might include the classroom teacher, the bus driver, the school guidance counselor, and the principal.

There were many times when the parent would be extremely embarrassed. They were then told, "This is what kids do; children try the system. Now it is up to us (indicating the parent, the teacher, and the principal) to teach the children that this is not acceptable behavior. Punishment is not needed this first time, but consequences are. Sit down with the children and brainstorm alternate ways of handling the situation. Allow the children to devise positive options for the next time."

However, if it happens again, punishment should be forthcoming. This system usually works. But this does not mean that choosing other options will transfer from this incident to the next. This system will need to be used more than once to become a way to positive behavior.

Whatever the child's learning style, guidelines are helpful in working toward and meeting them with success.

- Set goals. They need to be specific, in written form, and have a time limit; they should also be positive and realistic. They need to be measurable; that is, "How will the children know when the goal has been reached and completed?"

16   *Chapter 2*

- Put the to-do list in writing: on paper, in a notebook, on your computer, on a bulletin board, on sticky notes stuck in a special place, or on a handheld device; do not allow the children to just put it in their mind.
- Prioritize the activities according to the children's learning style.
- Vary the tasks by both interest level and the degree of physical activity required.
- Study in a setting that is conducive to the learning style; at a desk, on the bed, outdoors, and with or without background music.

In the Home

Everyone who lives in the home is the "family," and each member has a responsibility to the whole. The adults have the larger and more difficult tasks, but children also need to do their part, however small. Explain to the children what their responsibility is to the welfare of the family and the importance of that contribution. What would happen if:

- the children did not put the silverware on the table for dinner?
- the children did not take out the garbage?
- the children did not feed the family pet?
- the children did not shovel the snow from the sidewalk?
- the children did not load the dishwasher (or unload it)?
- the children left towels and dirty clothes on the bathroom floor?
- the children did not put their dirty clothes in the selected place for laundry pickup?
- And the list goes on.

These are the causes. A discussion of the effects will bring an understanding and awareness of the importance of the tasks. At that time, set up consequences. Now the hardest part: do not let the children "off the hook" (unless, of course, they are ill). Rules need to be put in place for what to do in case of a conflict of activities or events; for example, trade jobs with another family member. It is the children's responsibility to make the arrangements.

In the World

Extensive research carried out in many parts of the world has shown with all clarity that employers are now looking for different qualities in their employees than they used to in the not-so-distant past. What they are now looking for in the people they employ, is their ability to:

- Deal effectively with change.
- Keep learning new things and know how to learn.
- Think independently, both logically and creatively.[1]

Logic: The Rationale

By beginning to train children in the skill of logic in their early years, the children are being prepared for a lifetime. The training of any skill begins with an orientation, includes much mentoring and modeling, and encompasses years of practice to reach the level needed for success in the workforce.

In School

Teaching the skill of *cause and effect* is in every level of the elementary school curriculum. The content in the textbooks is the basis for discussion and analysis of the material. Each area of the curriculum is taught as an entity in itself, but many lessons lend themselves to interweaving with other subject areas.

Reading

The following types of questions are integral to the level of understanding for the "Why?"

- Why did _____ do _____?
- _____ happened. What would you have done so there would have been a different ending?
- What other options could the character have chosen to prevent _____ from happening?
- Some events have a chain reaction. What happened to the character to make him do what he did?
- (Example): _____ happened in the story. *The doorbell rang.* What effect did that have? *The dog started barking and running around the room.* What effect did that have? *As mom went to answer the door, she tripped over the dog.* What effect did that have? *She broke her arm when she fell.* And the scenario continues.

Social Studies

Studying history and geography mostly comprises learning about the events, why they happened, and what the effect was in the scheme of things. Cause and effect can be charted in a time line of events illustrating the chain reaction. This also brings an understanding to the student that no deed, event, or person stands alone, and that success is the result of that interdependency.

Begin with where the children are in their maturity. For example, field trips for young children are to the fire station, the police station, the airport, or the grocery store, all demonstrating the workings of a community. Older children visit museums, special concerts and plays for children, and landmarks and historic sites in their state; high school students

18   *Chapter 2*

take trips to the state capital and many go to Washington, DC. They see firsthand the effects of the past causes.

Math

Cause and effect is relevant when solving word problems in math. The word problem relates a scenario (cause). Then it will say "How much . . . " or "How many . . . ," and the student is required to use the information to solve the problem (effect). Students who are competent in solving computation problems (using numbers only) may have difficulty with the word problems. Word problems require more than just computation skills; they combine the three areas of elementary school math; concepts, computation, and application.

- Example: "There are twenty-six students in this classroom. Twelve brought their lunch from home today. How many students are buying their lunch today?"
- Concept: The student uses numeration and number relationships, identifying the key words and numbers in the problem.
- Computation: The student takes that information and decides which process is needed: addition, subtraction, multiplication, or division.
- Application: The student then applies the information to solve the problem.
- There are three skills involved: logic, particularly sequence of steps; next, the reading level of the student; and finally, the student's math computation skills.

Science

This is cause and effect and will be discussed in greater length in the chapter on experimenting. Remember, these five skills are entities unto themselves as well as skills that rely on and interact with each other.

SUMMARIZING

Summarizing is the skill of highlighting the main points of a story, event, or situation. Determining the main points or main idea is a skill that takes time and practice to master. Children relate their favorite part, not necessarily the main idea. The ability to do this is based on full comprehension of the subject at hand. Many terms define this skill: bottom line, get to the point, cut to the chase, outline, run down, and rehash. Sometimes it depends on their point of view. If children are asked, "What did you do at the birthday party?" their response might be "ate ice cream" (if it was someone else's party) or "opened presents" (if it was their own party).

Summarizing also includes sequence, that is, a step-by-step account of the story or event citing the important parts from start to finish. It is also needed in the other four learning skills. In order to summarize a story or event, the person has to comprehend and understand the event. A summary may be constructed by answering these questions: "who" (characters), "what" (event or circumstance), "when" (time frame—especially history), "where" (setting), "why" (the tough question—takes logic, critical thinking, and problem solving), and sometimes "how" (conclusion or strategy).

At Home

When working with children on this skill, ask specific questions that cannot be answered with "yes," "no," or "nothing." Examples: (1) "What did you do at school today?" You guessed the answer: "nothing." (2) "What story did you read at school today?" (3) "Tell me about your math lesson." (4) "What game did you play in recess?" (This question may be followed up with "What position did you play?")

After you read children a story, or when they read it to you, ask questions that will cause them to reply with a step-by-step summarization. Example: If you ask, "Tell me about the story," children will relate the parts they liked the best. If you ask, "Tell me three things about the story," children will respond with three events that may or may not be in sequence. Then ask, "What happened first, what happened next, and then what happened last?"

This is not a formal reading lesson; rather it is a fun, get-together time between parent and children. Show your approval of the children's responses, and if they missed an important point, tell them that you liked another part, too. Then discuss it. Use gestures and voice changes to illustrate your point. This is teaching, but children won't see it as a school lesson. Learning a skill takes continued practice, so look forward to many fun times.

In the World

Summarizing also means condensing facts to highlight the major points. It may even be a form of assessing or critiquing. In this world of technology, summarizing takes on a new dimension. Many folks do their shopping online. Each product on the Web has a section for reviews. These will be especially helpful to children in learning the skill of summarizing and when deciding which book, toy, or DVD to buy. A summary of a product can make or break a sale. A great deal of care needs to be taken to write facts about the product. Opinions are not part of a summary.

20   Chapter 2

The book *Charlotte's Web* had 150 reviews listed on one site on the Internet. One review said, "It was good. I liked Templeton the best because he was funny. I liked it." Another review said, "It was about the friendships and adventures of farm animals. The story revolved around three animals in the barnyard growing up and facing real life lessons, just as people do." Children like to write these and see their name on the website. Use this opportunity to have some together time and guide the child into writing a meaningful summary of the book.

People have the opportunity to e-mail government representatives about various issues, and many do so regularly. Many of their websites limit the space and number of words the writer may use. Thus, there arises the need for skills in writing summaries of the issue in order to state the important facts in as few words as possible. Again, time and practice are needed for mastery of this skill.

In School

Reading and social studies/history are the two subject areas that utilize summaries as a method of comprehending the material. After reading a story, article, or passage in any of the textbooks, the student generally is required to answer comprehension questions in writing. Copying a sentence from the text or paraphrasing what is written in the text does not signify that the student understands the material. To demonstrate mastery of the material (print form, stage or movie performance, or any live event) the student needs to be able to recap the information in as few words as possible.

Teachers teach this skill through book reports, presentations, group projects, and interpretations of time lines and graphs. Their first step is to teach the skill within the material in the classroom. The more difficult task, which only comes through practice, is to teach the students to transfer the skill to situations outside the classroom.

After the Christmas holidays, a first-grade teacher arrived at her classroom with a very excited first-grade girl waiting at the door. The teacher unlocked the door, they both entered, and the girl followed the teacher right to the closet where she hung her coat. Before the teacher even began to take off her coat the girl asked, "Guess what?" She did not even wait for an answer. "I can read!!!"

The teacher replied, "Of course you can, Susie. You are starting your fourth reading book today."

"No, I don't mean in school," the student answered. "I mean, I can really, really read. My dad was reading the newspaper and I looked at it and saw five words I could read!"

This student had made the discovery that there is no separation of inside school and outside school. It was quite a revelation, both to her and to her teacher.

Logic: The Rationale

PREDICTING

In order to predict what will happen, or what an outcome may be, the student needs to first evaluate what happened in the past, assess what is happening now, and then select attributes of all five skills that are necessary for making the prediction for the future. Actually, predicting follows sequence, cause and effect, and summarizing. It is important to teach children the difference between predicting based on fact or based on a dream. Example: Fact: If children do not study and hand in class work and homework, they can predict that they will get a low grade on their report card. Example: Dream: I want to be a doctor when I grow up. Fact: If I want to go to college, I have to get good grades.

There is an abundance of information in this chapter. Read it, digest it, think about what may be of advantage at this time for you and your child, and store the rest away and do not feel guilty for not using it all now. These skills are taught over a long period of time in accordance with the child's growth and development. This book is a resource, to be used when needed for that "teachable moment."

NOTE

1. Hoffman, Eva. *Teaching Experience* magazine. Autumn 2003.

THREE

Critical Thinking: The Assurance

If I had asked people what they wanted, they would have said faster horses. — Henry Ford

"Thinking is often casual and informal, whereas critical thinking deliberately evaluates the quality of thinking. The ability to think critically involves three things:

1. A state of mind regarding something.
2. Knowledge of the methods of logical inquiry and reasoning.
3. Some skill in applying those methods."[1]

For the purposes of this book, critical thinking is the skill needed to consider the facts, then assess and evaluate the information. The next step is to use all you have learned to make a decision as to whether that information is acceptable, unacceptable, or yet to be determined. This skill does not naturally evolve with a child; it must be taught. The success of the teaching is that it be continuous and consistent. The "teacher" may be an educator, parent, coach, counselor, caregiver, or any other "stakeholder" in the child's education. Yes, "It takes a village to raise a child" (old African proverb).

In 1956, Benjamin Bloom headed a group of educational psychologists who developed a level of intellectual behavior important in learning. In 1990 a new group led by a former student of Bloom's, Lorin Anderson, updated the levels, called "taxonomy," to reflect relevance for the times. These six levels begin with the most basic and increase in complexity in conjunction with the child's growth and maturity. The list begins with the lowest level.

- REMEMBERING: Is the child able to recall or repeat the information?

- UNDERSTANDING: Is the child able to explain the ideas or concept?
- APPLYING: Is the child able to use or demonstrate the information?
- ANALYZING: Is the child able to compare, contrast, or differentiate the information?
- EVALUATING: Is the child able to access, defend, or judge the information?
- CREATING: Is the child able to construct or develop a new point of view?

Because of the children's learning styles, they may be able to accomplish this process in one area in more detail than another. For example, they may have a stronger understanding of mathematics than language arts, or vice versa. That's okay. Cultivate their strengths.

After reading *Charlotte's Web* by E. B. White, ask the children to "tell you about the book." "I liked the book. It was funny, I liked Wilbur best. My favorite part was when . . . " are common responses. Then ask questions that will build the critical thinking skills, such as

- Remembering: Who was the girl who first liked the pig? What was his name? Where did Wilbur go to live? What were the names of Wilbur's friends in his new home?
- Understanding: What is going to happen to Wilbur? Describe Wilbur, Templeton, and Charlotte. What does Charlotte do to help Wilbur?
- Applying: Draw a picture of the barnyard with the characters in it. Write a story about how Wilbur met Charlotte. Act out a scene as if you were Charlotte, or Wilbur.
- Analyzing: When did Templeton finally decide to help Wilbur? How did Charlotte show that she was a good friend? What plan did they use to convince Mr. Zuckerman to let Wilbur live?
- Evaluating: Why was Wilbur allowed to live? What traits did each character have that caused you to like or dislike him? You said the story was "funny"; what did you mean?

Remember the four-year-olds whose every other word was "Why?" The children have begun critical thinking. Build on this skill. Critical thinking skills may be developed by following this format. The questions may be asked in different sequence, and not all six are needed in each situation. Let your child be your guide.

DEVELOPING CRITICAL THINKING SKILLS

Table 3.1. Critical Thinking in Six Steps

Authenticate	WHAT is the proof of the information?
Basis	WHERE is the source of the information?
Cause (Motivation)	WHY is this evidence to be believed?
Decision Maker	WHO is the "expert" or "authority"?
Experience	WHEN do you trust your knowledge over this information?
Flexibility	HOW open are you to change or other options?

Critical thinking may be taught through the competencies of *key points or phrases, plot/theme,* and *purpose of author.* The skill of investigating (chapter 5) will aid the student in searching for and locating the relevant information. Critical thinking is needed in deciding what to do with all that information, in choosing what is and isn't apropos in this situation, and to bring an understanding to the subject matter being learned.

KEY WORDS OR PHRASES

The word "key" has many meanings, such as opener, passageway, code, access, guide, clarification, or description. When asked "What is a key?", the young child will answer, "That thing that opens or unlocks the door or starts the car." Just as a key opens or unlocks a door, a key word or phrase will open or unlock information.

Many techniques and activities in this book involve making lists or charts. The method is of your choosing and one that is applicable to your circumstances. Depending on the type of list or information, these are some options:

- Notebook paper filed in a binder
- Three-by-five cards kept in a recipe box or bound with a rubber band
- Any size spiral notebook
- Saved on the computer in a folder
- Saved in a handheld device

Remember, the method should fit the activity. For example, if the child is doing math homework and needs the list of key words for word problems handy, use some sort of paper system. It is important to vary the method. Young children are still developing fine motor and eye-hand coordination skills. Thus arises the need for activities using manipulatives such as pencils, markers, chalk, or crayons on some form of paper, marker, or chalkboard.

In the Home

Spend a day or two and try to think of as many items as possible that a key will open. One teacher did this in a second-grade classroom on a large piece of poster board. The students were allowed to use a marker to add suggestions throughout the day. It became quite a competition. Some ideas were quite creative, as in "a pirate's treasure chest" and "castle."

Move on to teaching that a "key" may also be a word or words. These are important words that tell us what to do or where to go. Begin with simple commands, such as feed the dog, comb your hair, or set the table. These words or phrases clarify the task directions for the children.

When children respond to an ad on TV, in a magazine, or on the Internet, use that incident to teach the critical thinking skills by critiquing the information. What were the key words or phrases? What excited the children to want the product or want to attend the event? What information is important but was not in the ad? Consider cost, safety issues, side effects, or nutrition facts. Then ask, "Is this something you (the children) really want?"

In the World

The activity in the home may be expanded into the activities in the world. The grocery store is a prime example. The product may say it contains the entire day's supply of fiber but fail to mention the sugar content is high. Many products fail to mention the high salt content. Before shopping for any product, teach the children to make a list of the ingredients or attributes that are important. Then when in the store, or when ordering online, check those issues. This is also the time to read reviews from customers to see whether or not your important issues are dealt with.

When car shopping, one potential customer shopped online first, in order to become aware of what was available and which model met the customer's needs. When reading reviews about the vehicle on the top of the list, the customer read one that gave the vehicle a very low rating. Why? The cup holder was not conveniently placed for easy access. In this customer's mind, that attribute did not warrant a low rating for an automobile. Remember, "authenticate."

Blogs, news articles, and websites are "opinions" and should be treated as such. These are more complex and difficult to critique for children. Let your children's maturity level and age be your guide when discussing these sources. For children to become proficient in critically examining information, they must begin with the lower-level skills in Bloom's

Taxonomy and cultivate a consistent use of and then mastery of the skill before moving to the more complex level.

In School

Many common key words or phrases add a dimension to the understanding of information and add "critical" to simple thinking. These are found in all areas of the school curriculum and transfer to home and the world. The following is a basic list with which to begin. Define, describe, elaborate, clarify, and add others as needed for your child in your situation. For example, when teaching "fantasy," use words with similar meanings, such as make believe, can't really happen, imaginary, unreal, legend, or myth. Others are:

- General: not, always, never, true/false, fantasy/reality
- Comprehension: main idea, theme/topic/all about, opposite, compare/contrast, alike/different
- Math: in all/total/all together, more than/less than, more/less, greatest/least, fewest/most, equal, words denoting size or number
- Other: words denoting sequence (begin, first, end, last), spatial relations (above, bottom, under, next to), and time (before, after, early, late)

The more information children have on a specific subject, the better decision they can make in the situation.

PLOT, THEME, STORY LINE, OR MAIN IDEA

Using the skill of logic, the student is able to summarize the print material, the incident, the event, or the issue at hand. The skill of critical thinking, the process of decision making, is then used to decide what to do with the material; that is, what benefit is this information? what is the next step? what are the options? This is the step in which students think before they act or "look before they leap."

The plot, theme, story line, or main idea represents the whole picture, the summary. Many important facts or details are to be considered in understanding the plot, theme, story line, or main idea. This support material is then used in evaluating what is at hand and drawing conclusions as to what to do next.

Consider this scenario: on the school playground, a group of students have formed a circle around two other students. The two students in the circle are standing face-to-face. Here are the details. Their faces look very angry. They are shouting. There is some finger-pointing and some clenching of fists. They are each being urged on by their friends in the background. Your child is present. First, this child must decide the gist (main point, summary, scenario) of the situation: there are two angry boys and an excited crowd. A fight may break out at any minute. Next, the child will need to consider the best course of action: the options.

1. The child can simply walk away from the scene, thus getting out of harm's way.
2. The child can stay with the group to see what the two boys will do. (If a fight erupts, bystanders may get hurt. Also, when the adult authority arrives, because of their presence, the bystanders may have violated school rules and may have to face some consequences.)
3. The child can try to calm the other participants. This may be possible if this child is bigger and older than the others or is considered a leader. This also may be possible if this child is a trusted friend of both participants. These are pretty big "ifs."

The decision comes from background experiences and being taught the skills of summarizing, assessing, drawing conclusions, and taking action of some sort. Begin teaching the skill with stories or events as early as kindergarten. For each situation, discuss several options. Young children are capable of selecting options. Remember, some tend to get dramatic, as in, "ground them for life!" or "make them do the chore they hate the most for the next year." Then consider each as to why it is feasible or not feasible for this particular situation even though it may have been effective in another situation. As stories and events become more complex, so will the critical thinking skill. It will take time, consistency and trial and error.

In the Home

Assessing the scenario (critical thinking skills) and deciding upon options (problem solving skills) are a combination of two skills working in tandem. The facts of the situation can easily be listed. The hard part is condensing the information into one sentence that indicates the type of action to be taken. Use the newspaper or the Internet for practice in this area. A headline for a newspaper article has to be a short, attention-getting summation of the article. The same is true of headlines on the Internet. Writing these involves an understanding of the article.

Use this material in two different ways. Read the headlines with your child and list a few ideas of what the article will really be about. Then read articles and construct your own headlines. For young children, the articles need to be short and in their interest range. In the same vein, create new titles for books children read or movies they see. Children can get quite creative, and sometimes their suggestions are funny. One teacher related an incident after she read the story *The Little Engine That Could* to her first-grade class. When she finished, one child said, "Why didn't

Critical Thinking: The Assurance

they name it *Go, Train, Go!"*? Different generations, different catch-phrases.

In the World

Children learn the skill of recognizing the main idea, topic, or what it is all about through their reading, a movie, or a DVD. But they also need to be able to transfer the skill to a different venue, that of an event or activity. In other words, assess the situation. Sometimes an action or reaction is required, and sometimes just an understanding of the situation will be needed. Two types of activities will help young children learn this concept of an activity.

After the event, ask the child to list the most important things that happened. Then narrow the list to the top three, and from these, create a statement that would portray the main idea or gist of what happened. This may be done through a written list, numbering what happened by its level of importance to the child. The same process could be done on the computer. Left-brained and right-brained children will handle it differently, but they both learn the skill.

Another activity, particularly enjoyed by the right-brained child, would be to capture the event on camera. The pictures would be taken by the child. Then put them on the screen and assess them in the same manner as you did the written list. The top three may be printed out, and this creative child could make a poster (one sheet of printing paper) of the event. There would be a title, the pictures, and captions of the pictures. Save it, along with others, in a scrapbook or notebook for a memory album.

In School

In addition to the activities that follow reading lessons, the social studies text is filled with material that is best remembered when condensed to brief accounts of the event in history. If some details are forgotten, a quick search on the Internet will offer many sources of the information. The main ideas may be captured through a written time line. Each child in the class would be assigned a different event and given one sheet of printing paper. The assignment would be to write the dates(s) at the top, draw the picture in the middle, and add two or three sentences (main idea) at the bottom. Then the class would put them in sequential order, tape them together, and put the time line on the wall; sometimes it will reach halfway around the room. If there are several children in the family, or a group such as a scout group, homeschool group, or Sunday school group, this activity helps the children teach each other what is important.

30   *Chapter 3*

AUTHOR'S PURPOSE

An author writes for a specific purpose. The important details in the writing are "keys" that "unlock" the reason or agenda of the writer. The writing may be in any form of print material, in any format on the Internet, or any presentation on stage or TV that results from a written script. We will discuss the whole picture first, then plan strategies beginning at the lowest level and moving to the highest level with the maturing of the child.

1. An author may utilize the process of writing with the purpose of *entertaining* the reader, which affords the reader a few hours of enjoyment into a different milieu. This may take the form of comedy, adventure, mystery, romance, science fiction, or a heartwarming story about friendships and relationships.
2. A writer, an expert in a particular field, may wish to share the knowledge of a particular subject to *inform* or *educate*. The material is predominantly factual and documented by other experts or personal experiences. This book is in that category.
3. There are authors who choose to write to *persuade* the reader to a particular viewpoint or specific action. Many speeches are written for this very purpose. The subject matter, which is mostly opinion with the backing of some facts, includes politics, religion, ecology, and theories of several subject areas.

The three purposes may be intertwined. Material may be written to inform with the purpose of persuading. Material may be written to persuade while also informing. Opinions may be written to seem factual, and facts may be skewed to validate opinions. An author may write to inform while entertaining, as in the historical novel. However, the skill of discerning the author's purpose can be taught in a very basic, simplified form, developing in complexity when necessary.

Learning to evaluate the author's purpose will benefit the child in life. There are several activities appropriate for the young child. As early as the first-grade level, in reading tests accompanying the basal reader and also some national and state assessment tests, questions are asked about the purpose of the author. Sample question format might be:

- What was the author trying to show by . . . ?
- What is the purpose of the author in writing this story?
- When the author said _____, what did he mean?
- What does the author believe about the subject of a passage or the story?

Each question is followed by four answers, and the children select the correct one. They are not open-ended questions. The process for determining the author's choice is to follow the six steps listed for developing critical thinking skills.

In the Home

In first grade, children begin writing stories (some only four or five sentences) and book reports. This is the starting point for the teacher or parent. Read what the children wrote, then ask, "You wrote ____ . What did you mean by that?" The children may have said, "The book was funny." That could mean many things, but the children can readily explain what they meant.

Compliment the children on what they wrote, using such words as "author" (You are a good author. I like what you write.) and "purpose" (Now I understand the purpose of what you wrote. I know why you think it is funny.). After the child learns "author" and "purpose," begin to use these questions when discussing books read together. Also, when children bring home a library book, read it and then question them in the same way. Use this opportunity to show the children you are just curious and want their opinions of what they read. The children won't liken this activity to a "school lesson" even though they are learning a new skill.

As you watch TV or surf the Internet together, discuss the ads. Someone wrote them with a purpose in mind. By discussing the purpose, the child develops the ability to critique the words and the product.

In the World

The activities done at home and at school will generally involve books and ads pertaining to children. This skill prepares them for the future with more complex situations in which they may listen to a politician or "expert" in any field and assess what they heard. Activities for upper elementary–age children may include judging the purpose of the author of material (speeches, news reports, editorials) on TV, in newspapers, or on the Internet.

Another activity is to do Internet research on the books the students are currently reading. Read the reviews. Then judge whether or not the author of the review actually understood the purpose of the author. It is surprising what some people write. This skill of understanding the author's purpose is critical for children growing up in this age of technology, for they are inundated with all points of view daily. A lengthy discussion is not needed; keep it short and simple and stick to the most important facts in the information.

32   *Chapter 3*

In School

Language arts, which includes reading and writing, is the curriculum area used for teaching this skill. When children write a story, they have something to say: they have a purpose. That is where to start. The topic assigned by the teacher for youngsters is usually broad. The process the children use to select the specific topic will help them define their purpose. The assignment may be, "Write a story about a friend." This is the first step, called a prewriting diagram:

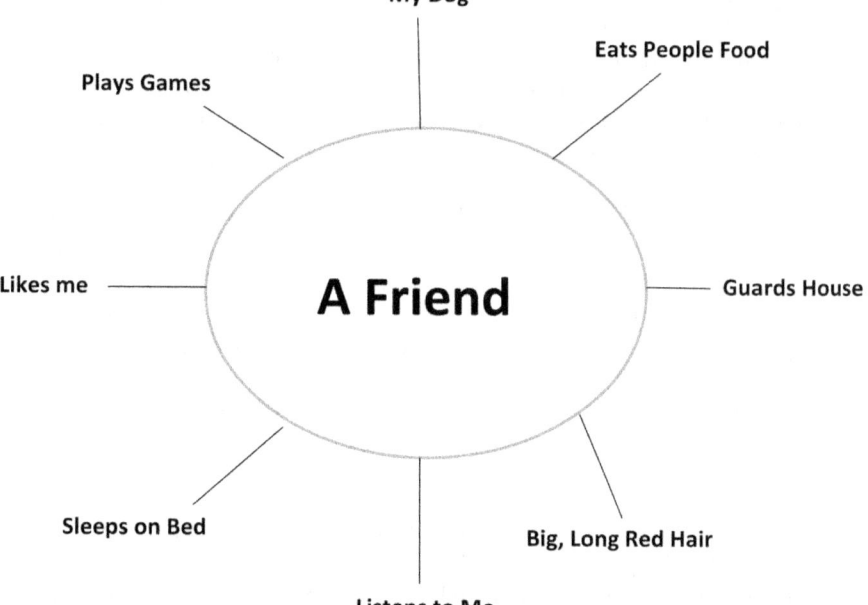

Figure 3.1.   **Prewriting Diagram.** *Created by Guinevere Durham*

The children write as many words as they can think of about the subject. The story line then emerges, as does their purpose: to tell the reader about their best friend, their dog.

Using the three competencies of critical thinking (consider the facts, assess, and evaluate) will help the child assess the information and draw a conclusion about the issue. Drawing a conclusion means using the information that is available (what you know) and considering what is implied (but not stated). Critical thinking is what takes the children beyond what is there and aids them in using good judgment skills in deciding what action to take, if any.

Some schools of thought believe that young children are not ready or mature enough to be taught critical thinking skills. Well, picture children throwing a temper tantrum. They have already learned that if they throw a tantrum, the parent will relent and give them whatever they want. They had assessed the situation, from past experience knew what was implied, and acted in a way that they knew would bring them the results they wanted.

Children are like sponges; they absorb what you give them. If they cannot absorb the lesson you are trying to teach, save it for another day. Always have a plan B ready and match the lesson to the situation at hand. Relevancy is the key. If their thinking process is flawed in any situation, talk about what went wrong and discuss what other options may have been more effective. If they repeat the inappropriate behavior, then consequences are in order. Once they know that their decisions matter, they will use the process themselves and develop the skill more fully.

NOTE

1. Glaser, Edward M. *An Experiment in the Development of Critical Thinking.* Teachers College, Columbia University, 1941.

FOUR

Problem Solving: The Process

I haven't failed. I've found 10,000 ways that don't work. —Thomas Edison

A problem is an unsettled question. Another definition is that a problem is a "question raised for consideration or solution." Solving a problem means finding an answer, a clue, a key, an explanation, or a clarification. In the process of solving the problem, several different strategies may be considered:

- Gathering and assessing relevant information
- Coming to a conclusion or finding a solution
- Deciding the feasibility and appropriateness of the solution
- Checking standards in similar situations
- Being open-minded to other options
- Working with a team, when necessary, on more difficult or intricate solutions

Problem solving is not an entity unto itself. It involves using all four skills during the process: logic, critical thinking, investigating, and experimenting. From the beginning (discovering the problem), through the process (fact finding, assessing information) to the final outcome (decision), active participation is required of the children. Children will incorporate their learning style to help them arrive at a solution that meets their needs in that situation at that time. What is important is that the children learn strategies and techniques for solving problems.

Another issue to deal with is that of timing. Some problems need immediate attention. Who can forget the words, "Houston, we have a problem"? That was critical and involved many experts. Fortunately, it had a happy ending. Some problems need to be handled immediately because of medical issues. Take care of that first, then sit down to assess what happened and why. Work with the children to decide other options on the issue of safety.

But the word "problem" does not necessarily denote negativity. It may simply mean that there are decisions to be made that take critical thinking. For children, the problem may be what brand or style of sneakers to pick out. It is a big decision for some young folks.

Issues such as selecting sneakers are lessons that help prepare children for more pressing situations. Being proactive and teaching them "negotiation skills" may deflect problems in the future. For instance, two siblings want to watch a movie, but they each want their favorite. Since this is typical family happenings, have rules and guidelines already in place for taking turns and sharing. If need be, put them in writing and make a contract for each to sign. That makes it official, and neither can say, "You never told me that." The important part of this is that the children help make the rules and begin learning problem solving skills.

An important concept in the problem solving process is that deciding the solution does not mean everyone involved "gets what they want." It means everyone works together for the common goal and arrives at a decision "everyone can live with."

A second-grade teacher had taught a lesson on "following directions" for the upcoming national assessment tests. The students completed several activities in following both oral and written directions exactly as stated. The teacher gave the students a teacher-made test. She told them that she would give two grades for the test, one for the correct information and one for following the directions. In one section of the test the directions stated, "Read the story and underline every noun." One student circled the nouns and thus received an A for correctly identifying the nouns and an F for not underlining them as the directions stated.

The next morning the child's mom arrived at the principal's office very upset. She said, "The nouns were all correct, so my son earned an A for the lesson." The principal explained the purpose of the lesson and how important it is to follow the directions exactly. On the standardized tests, graded on a machine, the response is either right or wrong; there are no gray areas. The mom "lived with" the explanation because she knew it was in the best interest of her son. The boy was a very good student, learned his lesson well, and scored extremely well on the national tests.

Three steps to consider when solving a problem are:

1. Identify the problem: The boy received an F for what seemed to be correct.
2. Assess the information: The lesson had two parts, English and following directions.

3. Draw your conclusion: Mom realized the boy deserved the F at that time in order to learn to do well on future tests and other assignments.

Throughout this book there are many techniques and strategies to consider when solving problems. The key is to select what is best in each situation. Sometimes it will be a matter of trial and error. That's okay. Always have a plan B ready. The competencies of particular importance in solving problems are *making inferences* and *decision making*. The other four skills also will contribute strategies to use in this area.

Solving word problems in math is difficult for many elementary school children. If the problem is set up as a computation problem using the correct format with just numbers, children are able to compute. However, when the problem is set up with words and children have to decide which numbers to use and, more importantly, identify the process, confusion arises. First, children need to look for the "key words," that is, the words that tell what the process will be (addition, subtraction, multiplication, or division). See Table 4.1. Some more complex word problems will have two steps using two different applications. For our purposes, for the young children, consider the following for where to start. Strategies for solving word problems are:

- Read the problem slowly and carefully.
- Eliminate unnecessary information.
- Highlight the key words.
- Identify the process (addition, subtraction, multiplication, division).
- Make sure units of measure throughout are the same.
- Compute the problem.
- Is the answer reasonable?

MAKING INFERENCES

Making inferences means deciphering what was implied but not said. This is commonly referred to as "reading between the lines." Think of "inferring" as reasoning, calculating, imagining, judging, guessing, suggesting, or putting two-and-two together, all to reach or arrive at a solution. Children may not understand this definition, but they will understand "What do you think?" and "What do you know?" in order to put it in a mathematical equation:

The stated facts + previous knowledge = Inference

For example: (1) Stated fact: one of your adult children telephones you; (2) Previous knowledge: you recognize the tone of voice and vocabulary; (3) The inference you make immediately is that the child has some sort of

38　　　　　　　　　　　　　　　*Chapter 4*

ADD SUBTRACT MULTIPLY DIVIDE OTHER

Table 4.1.　Key Words for Math Word Problems

Plus	How many less	Times	Divided into	Equal to
In all	How much less	Each (every item)	What fraction	Most
Total	How many left	How many in all	What part	Least
All together	Minus		Average	First
Join	Less than		Same in each	Between
Greater than	Difference		Each (one item)	Last
Sum	How many more needed		Everyone gets one	

problem and has called for advice, needs another viewpoint, or simply needs a listener.

Children learn to make inferences at a young age, even if they do not understand what they are doing. This is evident when they are choosing friends and playmates. They watch the other person's body language, listen to tone of voice and words spoken, and consider how that child relates to them.

Children see and hear the facts, remember previous situations, assess the situation, and make a decision as to whether or not another child will make a good friend. If you ask children why they like or do not like the other person, they will usually respond in reference to themselves, as in "I don't like them" or "They don't like me." They have judged the positive or negative traits to make their decision, but as yet, do not have the vocabulary to put it into words. This is the time to discuss specifics and teach the words that describe both the positive and negative traits.

First, ask children to describe what the other person did; for example, kicking, crossing arms, putting hands on hips, clenching fists, finger-pointing, smiling, offering to share a toy, or taking hold of the other's hand to bring that child into the group. Then begin talking about words that describe their traits.

- *Positive traits*: caring, kind, obedient, loyal, smart, brave, cautious, trusting, optimistic, creative, carefree, open-minded, loving, helpful
- *Negative traits*: uncaring, critical, bullying, defiant, controlling, manipulative, disloyal, not sociable, impulsive, selfish, pessimistic, reckless, mean, destructive, stubborn

Some of the traits can be either positive or negative, depending on the situation and the type of person to which children respond.

Problem Solving: The Process   39

Young children can be very literal in their approach. They do not know about making inferences, they just know (gut feeling?) that they do not like the other person. Learning to look for specific traits will help children develop good judgment in their associations with others. But they are still young. Don't analyze the situation too deeply; rely on age and maturity.

Follow this up with discussions about books, movies, or TV shows they watch. These are the teaching moments. When selecting books or DVDs for children, vary the selection. Choose stories about rural or big-city life, settings in foreign countries, settings in hot or snowy climates. The children know the facts about their friends and their own community. Help them to branch out to realize that it is okay to be different. Keep these questions in mind:

- What do you already know?
- What else do you need to know?
- What are the facts?
- What is the background knowledge (child's previous experiences in a like setting)?
- What information is important?
- What information is not important?
- What is the solution?
- What were the best clues that helped in the decision?

Children are developing problem solving skills by thinking about "Why?" and "What comes next?"

In the Home

Checkers. Imagine, this age-old game is great for teaching how to make inferences; in other words, "think before you act." Even the right-brained children, who tend to be impulsive, will learn strategies to help curb the behavior of "act, then think." As you play, let the children make their move, then ask, "Are you sure that is the move you want to make?" Another term to begin to use is, "Is that the best option?" They will begin to anticipate your question and take more time to assess the board and think before moving a checker.

This game is inexpensive, helps the child bond with family members, and promotes vocabulary. Buy other board games in which children have to interact with a live person, not a computer screen.

Young children read or listen to a story and respond to the actual words or actions. They haven't yet learned to think about what has not been said when considering their interpretation of the material. As you share a story in a book, on TV, or on a DVD, pause periodically to ask probing questions that will cause them to consider what is there and what they know from experience. Possible questions to ask are (1) Why did the character (or animal) do that? (2) What else could the character have done? (3) What would you have done? (4) What do you think will happen next? and (5) What were other options? (Ask this one at the end of the story.)

This interaction between parent and children (or between an older sibling or other caregiver) is instrumental in developing vocabulary, relationships, and thinking skills. Technology is great and has an important place in children's lives, but it cannot replace the opportunity for children to talk "with" another person (active) rather than listening to a technological device talk to them (passive).

Children are a member of a family and, as such, need to contribute to the welfare of all. Young children have a small role, which increases with age. For example, the five- or six-year-old may be responsible for putting the silverware on the table for meals. They are learning that everyone has to do their fair share and that they are responsible for their own actions.

Believe it or not, this lesson also teaches making inferences. If children forget to do their job, or choose not to, do not do it for them. When the food is ready and the dishes are in place, call everyone to sit for the meal. Of course there will be no silverware, so everyone will just sit (other siblings may make derogatory comments) and look toward the person in question. Ask them, "Why did I ask you to put the silverware on the table?" Fact: The silverware is not on the table. Implied: Silverware is needed in order to eat a meal. Conclusion for the children: I have to do my job of putting out the silverware or we will not be able to eat.

This is a simplified version of the concept, but it is a place to start. Use similar projects to prove the point, such as feeding a pet, taking out trash, putting dirty clothes in the designated area so they can be washed, or putting homework in the backpack ready for school the next day.

In the World

No area of the world is immune to natural disasters. The issue at stake here is survival. Children have most likely experienced one or another of the effects of nature's wrath. They have also witnessed their families preparing for the oncoming event. Sometimes the event gives little warning; thus, preparedness has to be taken in anticipation of the catastrophe. Fact: The children either have experienced or seen pictures on TV of damage done by a hurricane, tornado, or other disaster. Implied: Less harm came to those who took precautions. Conclusion: My family needs to protect itself from harm.

Not fully understanding what is happening and why the adults are so upset is unsettling to the children. Allow the children into the preparation and teach them what their role is in the family during this emergency. The emergency management office in your area has literature specifically prepared with guidelines and lists of safety measures. Discuss the literature concerning the children's environment with them, as well as stories of disasters in other areas as seen on TV. As you discuss procedures, ask why the people did what they did. Discuss how they might have felt when losing their home and what options they have next.

For example: Ask the following questions, in this case for a hurricane. (Answers in italics are those a child might say.)

- What do you already know? *Hurricanes are rain and very strong winds. They blow everything outside that is not nailed down all over. They blow trees over, blow out windows, and blow shingles or even roofs off houses.*
- What do you need to know? *How do I keep safe?*
- What information is available? *The police, firemen, and other people tell us what to do to be safe.*
- What information is important? *We need to board up the windows of the house. Everyone in the neighborhood does it. We need to get a generator to keep the refrigerator, air-conditioning, and lights working when the electricity goes out. Candles and flashlights are also helpful. We need to get lots of bottled water and food that won't spoil and that we can eat cold. SpaghettiOs are still good that way, but we need the old-fashioned can opener. We need flashlights and extra batteries. And I need to pack my duffel bag with pajamas and extra clothes in case we have to leave in a hurry to go to a shelter.*
- What are the best clues to decide the solution? *Things people did at other times that worked, are the best ones. Those are the things they told us on TV and we read in the booklets.*

Similar strategies may be used for other events in the community. Anywhere a crowd gathers for a specific purpose, such as a sporting event, a fair or circus, a school program, or holiday events, the children will witness and may be a part of inappropriate behaviors. "Reading between the lines" now becomes "reading the crowd." Teach children to assess the facts, think about what they know about body language and similar past incidents, and come to a conclusion as to whether it is okay to stay, move to a different area, or leave entirely and summon help. This skill helps children avoid being in the wrong place at the wrong time.

IN SCHOOL

Children begin to learn the skill of making inferences in the language arts section of the curriculum. The activities involved include using context clues to figure out an unfamiliar word, identifying character traits, and describing the setting. This information, in addition to the children's background knowledge, contributes to assessing and understanding the material. Using all three modalities in teaching the understanding of the

42   *Chapter 4*

reading passage is a way of reaching all students, regardless of learning style. Guide the children in completing the chart:

Character	Facts from story	What I know	Inference
First person			
Second person			

- *Auditory*: Discuss the first person. Ask for words that describe the character, both positive and negative. List these separately on the board.
- *Visual*: Tell the students to read the list and decide which words best describe that character.
- *Kinesthetic*: Select students to come to the board to write their selections in the chart.

Follow the format with any other characters, then with "what I know," and finally with the inference. Allow the spaces to be big enough to accommodate the children's handwriting. Another way to do this is to give a sticky note to each child, one for each character in the discussion. The children will write one word or phrase about the character. Have each student in turn stick their note on the marker board. One basic rule of thumb is to tell the students that every idea is accepted, for it is that child's opinion. There will be absolutely "no put-downs." This type of lesson is time-consuming but so rewarding, even for first- and second-graders.

Social studies is another area of the curriculum that requires the skill of making inferences to understand the material. November projects usually involve the study of the Pilgrims and culminate in a feast of some sort in the classroom. Even young children can recite the facts: (1) Pilgrims dressed in black with some white. (2) They lived in log homes. (3) They went hunting for food. (4) They had gardens and grew vegetables. (5) They were friends with the Indians and had a feast together. The students are too young to have experienced the whys of these facts. This is the beginning of their education of the "what I know" part of the making inferences skill.

One celebration in a rural school was quite interesting. The teachers all talked of their "feasts" in their classrooms the day before the Thanksgiving vacation. They planned activities the same as they had in previous years. The feasts were to be held on a Wednesday. On Monday and Tuesday the principal witnessed parents bringing in bread, cookies, fruits, pies, cakes, and even an uncooked turkey.

On the day of the feast, the new female principal took a walk-through in all the rooms to witness the celebrations. As she entered a fifth-grade

Problem Solving: The Process   43

classroom, two boys came up to her, and each said, "We had four kinds of pies, and I ate a piece of each. I'm stuffed!" The only thing they learned was what good cooks their moms were. The next year she created different ground rules. They could have their feast, but any food they ate had to be cooked in the classroom. What a difference. There was pumpkin pudding, applesauce, bread, oatmeal cookies, corn on the cob, freshly churned butter, and homemade ice cream.

The cafeteria served the traditional dinner that day with the turkey. The feasts were the afternoon fare. The ovens in the cafeteria were available to the teachers. Some retired dads and granddads brought charcoal grills and manned them for roasting the corn on the cob. This time when she took her walk-through, the students said, "We made this. It is so-o-o good. You have to try some." They had constructed homes from Lincoln Logs, made Pilgrim hats from construction paper, and made Indian headdresses, complete with feathers. The next year they had their facts, but also some experiences to draw from.

This skill of making inferences is needed in the science curriculum. It is taught during all the cooking lessons, especially when using yeast. There is more on science in the chapter on experimenting.

DRAWING CONCLUSIONS

A "conclusion" may be defined as an accomplishment, a fulfillment, a climax, a summary, a wrap-up, a result, or a final decision. To arrive at the point of drawing a conclusion, the students have much work to do. They begin the process using logic and critical thinking and then arrive at the heart of the matter through their inference-making skills.

This process is a learned activity, and each step is a prerequisite for the next. All steps are important. An important concept to be taught at this point is the term "jumping to conclusions"; include some examples. Discuss past decisions and how and why the person arrived at that conclusion. We make decisions with the facts and with what we know at the time. At another time, the decision may be different. Thus, every step counts.

The difficulty of following the process in drawing conclusions for children is that they have not yet acquired a wealth of experiences and background knowledge. The children build these experiences through varied activities and expand their limited environment through books and movies. A classic example is the story "City Mouse and Country Mouse," in which each visits the other and comes away from the experience with the thought, "It's a great place to visit, but I would not want to live there." But, more importantly, each experiences a world outside their own, which adds to their knowledge base.

44   *Chapter 4*

With the youngest of children, begin the naming of items or actions with the proper words or phrases. For example, a dog is not a bow-bow, a truck is not a vroom-vroom, and an item that children want is not an eh-eh (accompanied by a pointing finger). Simply say the correct term, "that is a truck," and it does make a noise like "vroom-vroom." This is said as a statement of fact, not as a criticism. The important skills for the parent are patience and repetition, much repetition. A college professor was noted for telling teachers in an education class, "The brain can absorb only as much as the bottom can endure. Take breaks as needed."

Children have now accomplished the first three steps of solving a problem: (1) identifying the problem, (2) citing the facts, and (3), bringing what they know into the equation. The next step is to formulate options, citing at least three. First, brainstorm every idea that comes to mind, even if it seems ridiculous.

Write each on a sticky note and stick it on the table where you are working. Again, follow the rule for this process; that is, there are no put-downs. The process will take care of eliminating inappropriate ideas in a logical way. Compliment the children on their creativity and good thinking skills. Using paper and some sort of writing instruments, involve the children physically as well as mentally, not with the click of a mouse or flick of a finger.

Next, eliminate the choices that the children have realized will not work. This will take some time. It is wise to limit the children to no more than five or six suggestions, for the facts and background knowledge of each have to be discussed. One easy visual way to do this is to use the schematic in chapter 3. On a sheet of paper, draw an oval in the middle of the page and stick one of the notes in it. Allow the children to draw the lines from the top of the oval upward, listing the facts. Then draw the lines from the bottom down, listing the known information. There will be one sheet per idea. Then start eliminating those that are not feasible for any number of reasons. These are some questions to ask:

- Do I need help to do this?
- Is the help available?
- Are others involved in agreeing to the solution?
- What is my role in the solution?
- Will it cost money?
- Is this a solution or a conclusion?

A conclusion may be a decision arrived at through the facts and background knowledge. A solution generally involves several steps of action and may include others in the handling of the situation. A situation in which children work alone would be in selecting an answer to a multiple choice question on a test. A situation in which children may need the help of others is that of handling a bully who only causes problems when no adult is nearby.

Problem Solving: The Process   45

In the Home/In the World/In School

Many of the problem solving activities and strategies already listed may effectively be used at home, in the world, and at school. One particular area of concern for children that involves the skill of drawing conclusions is in taking tests. The national and state tests are scored electronically; thus, each answer is arrived at through selecting the best of four choices. The skills of logic, critical thinking, and problem solving will provide them with a strategy to use in this process.

Research has proven that test takers who have learned how to take tests will increase their score by 10 to 20 percent. That is because the test-taking anxiety has been alleviated, allowing the test taker to concentrate on the questions. There is an old saying, "You gotta have a gimmick." Well, this is one for remembering the process to select the one best choice for an answer.

S: State the *problem*
O: Obtain the *facts*
L: List *what I know*
V: Validate the *inferences*
E: End result—*draw conclusions*

Children in elementary grades can be taught this slogan and the meaning. First teach "solve." Most will know the word and understand the meaning. Then work on the five steps, explaining the words and using them often. Children learn vocabulary and word recognition by being exposed to it often.

There are three strategies to choose from: (1) narrow the choices to two and guess; (2) eliminate all the choices you know are wrong and guess from what is left; and (3) work backward and find the answer that fits the question. The following is an example of a test question and an explanation of how the process works.

Directions: Read the passage. Then read the question and choose the best answer. Fill in the space in the answer row that goes with the answer you have chosen.

> It was a windy day in March. Mom bought a kite for the twins, Emma and Nick. They wanted to put it together right away. Nick put all of the pieces on the floor. Emma got the string. Then she tore up an old towel for the tail. They worked fast and made a pretty red kite.
>
> Mom took them to the park. Nick tried to fly it first. It did not fly. Next Emma tried to fly it. It would not go up. Then they both held on to the string and ran as fast as they could. It flew! When the wind stopped, mom took them home.

What is the story all about?
   O 1.) *The kite was red.*
   O 2.) *Nick and Emma were twins.*
   O 3.) *Mom had brown hair.*

46   *Chapter 4*

O *4.) Kites are fun.*
Strategy to choose the correct answer:

S The problem is: "What is the story all about?" There is only one answer.

O The facts are: (1) It was windy. (2) Emma and Nick put together a kite. (3) They went to the park to fly it. (4) It flew.

L I know: (1) Kites need wind to fly. (2) You have to run fast to get them to go up. (3) I had fun when I flew my own kite.

V (1) "The kite was red" was just one part of the story.

(2) "Nick and Emma were twins" was only one part of the story.

(3) "Mom had brown hair" was not even in the story.

(4) "Kites are fun." They put it together fast. They worked together. It flew! All these choices showed strong feeling.

E Eliminate #3 because it was not in the story. Eliminate #1 and #2 because they only told about one part. So the answer is #4.

The test taker marks the space next to #4. As this process becomes more familiar to the children, they will work faster. These tests are timed, so the test taker must work at a steady pace in order to finish. Practice the process with homework selections in all areas of the curriculum.

FIVE

Investigating: The Clues

Supposing is good, but finding out is better. —Mark Twain

To investigate means to "search into" for the purpose of learning the facts. Other words for investigate are research, seek out clues, inquire into, check on or into, examine, analyze, look into, or inspect. This is the skill that is needed to help decide what is true or not true, fantasy or reality, or fact or opinion. It may be complicated and time-consuming and it may be developed through experiences and maturation.

Investigating is a necessary component of the other learning skills. It is used to validate the information in question. For young children, this concept cannot be considered without adult guidance. The following scenario is an example of the beginning of the process for a seven-year-old girl, Susan.

Susan lived in an area of a growing community that had just built another elementary school. Thus, the entire small district had to be restructured. Susan would begin second grade in a different school than the one she had attended. There was some apprehension.

After playing in the backyard with neighbor children, she told her mom, "Jimmy said my new teacher is mean." Jimmy had been in both kindergarten and first grade with Susan. She liked him but knew that Jimmy had a tendency to exaggerate. Her mom took the time to sit with Susan and go through a short, basic investigative process to decide whether or not to believe that the fact (as stated) was true. The answers to the questions are in italics.

- Who is the source of this information? *Jimmy's cousin told him. Bobby goes to that school.*

48   *Chapter 5*

- What did the teacher say or do that he thought was mean? *I don't know. I asked Jimmy because I wanted to know, but he said that Bobby hates school and does not like any teachers.*
- Was Jimmy or were any of his brothers or sister ever in this teacher's class? *No.*
- Did anyone else in the neighborhood say the teacher was mean? *No.*
- Did Jimmy say anything else bad about the teacher, or maybe anything good? *No, that's all he knew.*

Next, they considered the "what I know" issue.

- Does Susan like school? *Yes.*
- Does Susan get along well with her teachers and other children in the classroom? *Yes, Susan is friendly, caring, and has a good sense of humor.*
- Does Susan believe what Jimmy said is true or would she rather wait for school to start and find out for herself? Susan thought for a few minutes. *I like Jimmy, but I don't always believe what he says. Sometimes we don't even agree. Can we go meet her before school starts?*

A meeting was arranged, for the mom had to alert the teacher to a possible health issue Susan faced. That gave them an opportunity to meet the teacher. When they came away from the meeting, they discussed the issue of being "mean" again. They learned that the teacher was strict and demanded the very best from each child. She was fair and very experienced. Mom had asked the teacher to allow Susan to sit in the front row in order to hear, at least until October, for a hearing test was scheduled with a known specialist in the area. There was a concern about some hearing loss.

At that comment the teacher broke out into laughter. She said, "Of all the teachers to be assigned, I have the loudest voice. Some parents complained because my voice is too loud." Susan's comment on the way home was, "I liked her laugh. I think I am going to like being in her class." Incidentally, the teacher turned out to be one of Susan's favorites.

Young children deal with statements or comments from their peers that seem to be true. They need the adult to help them sort out fact from opinion. The important steps for this age child or younger, are deciding whether or not the source is believable and discussing the "what I know" section. As the children mature and deal with more complex issues, the basic knowledge is there in which to begin the investigative process and then to delve into it more deeply. Remember, all the skills in this learning process grow with the children in time, in complexity, and in comprehension.

The investigative skills discussed in more depth are *compare/contrast, fact/opinion,* and *fantasy/reality.* Some basic, elementary points of each may be used even with preschool children. Pick and choose what fits your child, in your situation, and you.

COMPARE AND CONTRAST

Compare, in this context, means to investigate two or more objects, events, places, people, or subjects in order to identify similarities or likenesses. To compare is to liken, match, equate, identify with, correspond, be on a par with, or be on equal footing. Words used with *compare* are: similar, like, likewise, in the same ways, in the same manner, or in comparison.

Contrast means to investigate to show differences or unlikenesses. To contrast is to part from, deviate from, contradict, counter, or stand apart from. Words used with *contrast* are: however, but, yet, on the other hand, nevertheless, rather, conversely, or on the contrary.

This skill is used to help students clarify ideas and differentiate places, people, ideas, or things. This is difficult for young children, as it requires them to evaluate and assimilate. Some examples listed below are effective for the beginning of the mastery of this skill. The simplest form is identifying the pluses and minuses of something the children want to own.

Compare/contrast is a form of classification. Activities teaching children to classify may be started as early as preschool. For example, place a fork, knife, spoon, and pencil on the table. Ask the children, "What does not belong?" If necessary, discuss what each item is used for and then repeat the question. Then ask the question, "What three things belong together?" Use items the children can actually touch. Later move on to pictures of items, and finally to printed words.

Children who participate in the decision-making process are more likely to accept the final outcome. That does not mean they will like the outcome, it means they understand why that particular decision had to be made. Actually sitting down together and completing one of the following activities helps children take ownership in the decision. Remember to vary the process. Sometimes a handheld device or small notebook will not display all the information the children need to visualize before them in order to compare characteristics. Acquaint them with several types of options available to them in making their decision.

There are three formats for this activity. The issue at hand will dictate which one is the appropriate selection for the activity. The examples are those that relate to children. They are the Venn diagram, the matrix, and the T-chart.

Creating the Venn diagram and then seeing it on paper or a screen in front of you will help in the decision making, sometimes far more realistically than if an adult just told these things to the children. Since the seasons are concurrent, the child can only join one sport, and the final decision has to be that child's decision. This same procedure can work for

50   Chapter 5

Figure 5.1.   Venn Diagram. *Created by Guinevere Durham*

comparing or contrasting characters in a story, places and customs discussed in social studies, and any number of issues with two sides to
consider.

MATRIX

This diagram is used to compare two or more items. It may be created in
the form of a table, chart matrix, or columns drawn on paper. One example is that of children trying to decide which musical instrument to learn
to play in the school marching band.

Down the left side of the page, list the issues involved: cost of instrument, lessons, uniforms, and shoes; transportation to and from lessons or
practices; issues with practicing daily in the home; and possible positive
outcomes (college scholarships).

Across the top of the page list the instruments. Draw lines down the
page to create columns. Do the same across the page to create separate
rows. The outcome is several boxes in which to write the information.
Then fill in the boxes with the information. The whole picture is in front
of the children. Highlight positives in one color and negatives in another
color. Then discuss the option that best meets their needs at the time.

- *Table, chart, or matrix*: In your Word program, click *insert*. Then
  select the options of table or chart to choose the format. Children
  like to create, especially when they are creating for a specific purpose. This format is a favorite with right-brained children.
- *Paper*: Use a sheet of printing paper and have the children use a
  ruler to draw lines to make columns and rows in which to write all
  the information. A sheet from a legal pad works well also. It already has rows or lines; the children simply draw the columns.

The third diagram is named for its configuration, a T-chart. It is used
to compare the pluses and minuses or pros and cons of an issue, event, or
object. It is very useful in helping the child evaluate and decide.

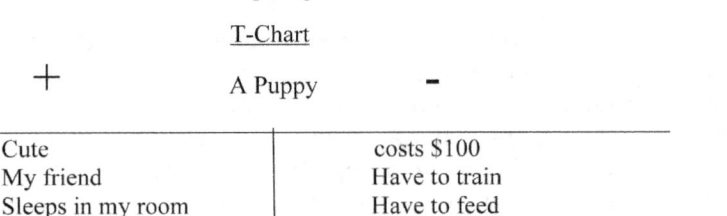

T-Chart

+ A Puppy −	
Cute	costs $100
My friend	Have to train
Sleeps in my room	Have to feed
Protects me	Food, supplies & Vet bills
I won't be lonely	Chews things
I will learn to be	Makes messes in the floor
responsible	Must be walked, even in bad weather

All three activities may be used at home, in the world, and at school. This process uses all three modalities. The child talks and listens to mom (or whoever is helping with the project), sees what is in writing or printed on the monitor, and actually writes or types the information. For the left-brained person, this list making is a natural procedure. The right-brained person will see the heading (the whole picture), and then as they deal with all the parts or pieces needed, they can write or type each item where it belongs. Both types of learners come to the same bottom line; they just take a different route. The information is there, but how do you know if it is true? That is the next step.

FACT OR OPINION

A fact is a statement of truth or actuality and can be proven. It is based on direct evidence, an actual experience, or an observation. A fact is true all the time for all people. An opinion is a statement of belief, judgment, or feelings. It tells someone's thoughts or opinions on an issue. An opinion is not true all of the time for all people.

Facts are not open to debate, and everyone who has the same information should be able to draw the same conclusion. For example, a teacher walks into her classroom and counts the number of students. There are twelve girls and ten boys. Anyone walking into the room and counting the number of students would come to the same conclusion. Facts can be verified, and they are expressed in concrete language or numbers.

Opinions can be identified by specific language or key words, such as *I think*, words pertaining to the five senses (It tastes . . . , it feels . . . , it smells . . . , it sounds . . . , it looks . . .), adjectives, adverbs, descriptions, or labels. Opinions are often expressed as comparisons. The same teacher who counted the students decides that there should be two more boys in the class. Everyone would agree that there are twenty-two children in the class (fact), but everyone would not agree that there should be two more boys (opinion).

The most important question to ask about the information is, "What is the source, and can it be trusted?" There are several avenues to pursue to prove the information: websites (two or more), public records, interviews (two or more), print material (books, magazines, journals, newspapers, almanac, dictionary, and encyclopedia), and observation/experience. The reference specialist at the local library has a wealth of information for locating specific information. Expose children to the multiple ways of proving the information and how to decide which ones are best for particular issues. This skill is needed for reports and research projects at school.

Using pictures from library books, magazines, or ads, ask children several questions and allow them decide whether the question is a fact or opinion. For example:

Fact questions:	Opinion questions:
1. There are 2 ???.	1. The girl is having a good time.
2. There is a ??? in the yard.	2. The boy is sad.
3. The boy is riding a ???.	3. The dog is mean.
4. The girl is wearing ???.	4. It is a warm day.
5. There are clouds in the sky.	5. The girl thinks her dress is pretty.

If the children agree with the information, they may also believe it is true, even if it is an opinion. The process of proof will help them distinguish between fact and opinion.

In the Home

Lessons learned at home are the ones that give children the tools they need to deal with unpleasant situations. For young children, that usually means bullies at school. These bullies know that the best way to antagonize their victim is to use name-calling, and the primary target is the child's mother. It is done outside earshot of any adult in the vicinity. It also may be said quietly enough that even other children in the vicinity will not hear it.

For example, Billy, a fifth-grader, was sent to the principal from the playground because he had hit another child (the bully). Billy was a very good student, well liked by his teachers and peers, caring and helpful, and usually the negotiator in these types of situations. The principal knew that he had been provoked beyond his tolerance.

To set the stage as to what the principal was seeing: Billy lived with just his mom, and they were struggling financially. His clothes were ill-fitting and worn, but always very clean. His mom always came to school

Investigating: The Clues   53

when asked, and it was obvious she loved her son and wanted the best for him. She was a large woman, and when she came to the school, she wore ill-fitting shorts (this was in the south), a tank top, and flip flops. Her hair was light colored, shoulder length, unwashed, and stringy.

The principal asked Billy to tell the story of what had happened. The principal was sitting behind the desk, and Billy was sitting on the other side just a few feet away from the desk. He sat on the edge of the chair, and his hands were in tight fists. This bully had been needling him for a few weeks.

Billy said, "He said my mom is fat and ugly!"

The principal responded, "Is she?"

Emphatically he answered, "NO!"

The principal then said, "Billy your mom loves you very much, she has a heart of gold, and she takes good care of you. You have every right to be proud of her. Now! Since what Joe (the bully) said is not true, don't let him get you this upset. You see, when a person wants to really get someone else angry, he knows all he has to do is call the other person's mom names. Joe did this. It worked, didn't it?" Billy nodded. The two of them then brainstormed some tactics Billy could use to verbally disarm the bully and defuse the situation.

Be proactive. Teach the following strategies to young children so they are prepared to cope with such situations, and in life there will be many. The format is whatever works best for you. Put two headings at the top of a sheet of paper, one saying "What someone says" and the other, "My response."

In the first column, list comments that children might hear, such as:

- You are ugly.
- You are fat.
- You are not a good ballplayer.
- You are stupid.
- You can't . . . .
- Your family is . . . .

Then discuss responses children might use in each situation and write them in the second column. These are some things students have told teachers that they have used with success.

Start with, "You have a right to your opinion, but I think my mom is the greatest." (Acknowledging the bully will surprise him.)

One student would tell the bully, "You are stronger than I am and I do not want to fight because I do not want to get hurt."

One fourth-grade girl would say, "If you say so." A tactic another student used was to shrug her shoulders and say "Whatever" and then walk away. Walking away when there are other people in the vicinity stops the bullies, for if the bully chases the victim and starts a fight, the bully is the one in trouble.

54   *Chapter 5*

Bullies are usually sneaky, especially if there are adults within eyesight. If the child hits the bully or shouts disclaimers, a fight will probably ensue and the bully will win. This strategy is not 100 percent foolproof, but it will help in many situations.

In the World

Another issue that comes into play here is that the comment may be true, but it is not important. The boy who was told that he is not a good ballplayer may know that the statement is true. However, he has no aspirations of being a great athlete. He joined the team for the comradeship of his teammates, some fun, and some exercise. He also knew that every team had star athletes, but the support players were equally important. With that knowledge base, the bully's comment was not as insulting as intended.

Again, consider the source and the reliability of the information. In the lesson above, this is a strong piece of the puzzle. When making the chart, discuss the importance of the strengths and the knowledge that his weaknesses may only seem as weaknesses to others. He can use his strengths to work with the weaknesses. This is the skill children need in order to thrive in the world.

Use the many sources available that were stated earlier in the chapter to prove whether or not the information is factual. Point out their strengths to the children. In this case it may be good grades, artistic or musical talent, their rapport with animals, their bicycle riding skills, and the list goes on. The key is that the children learn how to succeed using the skills that are their forte. What is taught in the home will follow them through life in the real world.

At School

In the classroom create a lesson in which the students learn information. Start by asking the students what information they would like to know. Put the comments on the board, on a chart, or use the sticky notes. Discuss whether the response will be a fact or an opinion. Questions may be some of the following, but every question is acceptable (unless it is too personal):

- How old is the school?
- How many students go here?
- How many classrooms are there?
- How long has their teacher taught at this school?
- Where is the principal from?
- Who is the best teacher?
- What is the favorite lunch item?

Investigating: The Clues   55

Young children will ask some very interesting questions. Divide the group into teams with a few questions each and tell them they have a week to find the answers. This format is more conducive to upper elementary students. Primary classrooms will be better served by doing the project as a classroom unit. They may interview staff members or the principal, look up information on the Internet or in the school library, or check old yearbooks. This activity would already have been cleared by those who would need to be involved.

Before sending the students to work, the group needs to decide whether each question will give an opinion or a fact. Some opinions may not be given readily, but this is a part of the learning process. Facts are easily shared (except personal ones), but some opinions are not.

The same process may be used in finding out information about issues in the social studies textbook or increasing and verifying information in a literature selection in their reader. This, however, may be through the research sources already listed in the chapter. Whatever the age of the child, mentoring and supervision are needed.

FANTASY AND REALITY

This category may also be called fiction versus nonfiction.

Fantasy is fiction, imagination, fancy, illusion, whim, vision, originality, inventiveness, and dreams. Myths, legends, fairy tales, and mysteries may also be considered fantasy. These cannot be proven.

Reality is nonfiction, actuality, truth, fact, and tangibility. Statements, whether spoken or in print form, can be proven through the process of investigation.

Differentiating between fantasy and reality is a process that evolves within the early childhood years. Understanding that concept precedes the concept of fact versus opinion. The year of the four-year-old is one of exuberance, enthusiasm, and out-of-boundness. It is also a year of storytelling with embellishment and exaggeration. When they tell a story, if they don't have all the facts or if they don't understand the facts that they have, the children just fill in the blanks as they see fit, and they believe what they say.

Their maturity level has not yet reached the stage where they can tell the difference between fantasy and reality or fact and opinion. They are not lying or "being bad"; they are simply being four-year-olds. This is the time for the adults in the children's lives to gently, but firmly and consistently, restate the truth of what the children have said while omitting the untruths.

By five years of age, the sense of fantasy versus reality begins to blossom. They still may tell tall stories, but with a twinkle in their eyes and a semblance of a grin on their faces, for they know they are fooling mom and dad. There are times they will make up a story or blame others for what they have done in order to protect themselves. They do not realize the detriment blaming someone else can cause.

One mom walked into the bathroom and caught her five-year-old daughter drawing a picture on the wall with crayons. The girl looked up at her mom and stated that her four-year-old brother had done it.

Mom replied, "He is taking a nap." The child thought for a minute and then said, "How about you!"

Mom found it difficult to keep from laughing. Instead, she filled a bucket with soapy water, gave the girl a sponge, and sat there to supervise the cleanup job. While the girl worked, Mom told her that blaming someone else for what she did was not being nice to them nor was it fair. Fairness is important to children. They will learn in time that the world is not fair. Even at five, a child will tune out long lectures or yelling.

Each year, through personal experiences followed by mentoring and evaluations of appropriate behavior, the child develops a sense of fantasy versus reality. Discuss what happened and point out the parts that are true (reality) and the parts that are not true (fantasy). As the child begins to understand the concepts, allow him to point out which parts are true and which are not. A strong mastery of the concept comes around the age of eight or nine. As with all learning, the concept of fantasy/reality evolves over time, sometimes years.

In the Home

Select a story of fantasy to read to the children. An example might be the *Curious George* books about the mischievous monkey. Then select a book that depicts the true information about the character; for instance, a book that tells about the life of real monkeys. Laugh together over the antics of Curious George, and then delight in what real monkeys are really like.

In the World

Many of these activities may be carried on at home or at school, but they concern holidays and events that are celebrated in the community and beyond. This is the time to introduce the terms "myth," "legend," and "tradition." In a second-grade classroom every December, one teacher created a unit called "Christmas Around the World."

Being in a public school, the religious aspect was a taboo subject. She concentrated on two aspects that were in the children's scope of the holiday: do the children in that country have a Santa Claus and do they hang up a stocking? She placed a large map of the world, four feet by eight feet, on the bulletin board in the back of the room. The major object of the lesson was to teach the students that everyone does not have the same

Investigating: The Clues

beliefs and customs, and it's okay. They learned that some customs were facts and some were fantasies.

The activities varied. The children made a piñata representing Mexico, a tradition the students thought was "cool." The teacher taught them the song "Rudolph, the Red-Nosed Reindeer," which many already knew. Then she read them a story about real reindeer, and the class visited the school library to find picture books of many kinds of reindeer. Even within the classroom were many different beliefs and customs. They drew pictures of a tradition in their own homes, which were then tacked up on the bulletin board around the map.

One of the highlights was the Christmas party for which the children had cooked all the goodies: piñatas filled with candy, Swedish Spritz-baaken cookies, Italian pizzelle cookies, German stollen bread, American popcorn balls, and the wassail drink from England. Another plus to these activities is that they learned an extensive vocabulary of cooking terms, and they learned how to measure. If you haven't watched a seven-year-old break an egg or watched the boys knead bread (with every ounce of strength in their bodies), you have missed one of the glories of childhood.

Before every school holiday, this same teacher taught the children about the origin and customs of it and why they were getting a day off. They did not have to believe in the customs or even celebrate the holiday or event, but they needed to know about what was happening in the world around them.

In School

Many of the holidays lend themselves to activities that not only help teach fantasy versus reality, but teach other concepts from the curriculum.

- One teacher wrote a story about the history of the jack-o'-lantern in second-grade vocabulary and copied it for each child for their reading lesson. Then they carved a pumpkin, discussing circles or triangles for the features. They baked the pumpkin seeds and then used the pumpkin the next day to make pumpkin bread.
- Another teacher created a unit on insects, and the students made a paper spider. It began with a four-inch square of black paper. There was quite a discussion on how to make a circle out of the square. Then the teacher gave each child four strips of construction paper (one inch by eight inches). They accordion-pleated the "legs" and stapled them to the "body." She then read them a story about real spiders called "Be Nice to Spiders."
- The students in another classroom made a paper black bat, but the pattern they were given was of half a bat. Again, it was quite a discussion about how to make the whole bat. There was a good

fifteen-minute film on file in the library that she showed, teaching what real bats were like.

Vocabulary, science, and math concepts are taught and remembered when the children learn them through a hands-on project. Much of the vocabulary may not be in the curriculum of a primary grade, but these words are in the child's real world. The child is more likely to learn the difference between fantasy and reality when they are exposed to both views through activities and the media. The Internet makes it easy to research the information that brings the concept right into the child's world. This is all fun time and bonding time.

SIX

Experimenting: The Proof

I hear and I forget. I see and I remember. I do and I understand. —
Chinese proverb

An experiment is a process or action undertaken to discover something
not yet known or to demonstrate something already known. This process
is used in many fields in the form of observing, studying, searching out,
or experimenting in order to determine the nature of what is being studied. The field of science as it relates to young children is the topic of this
chapter.

For children, the word "experimenting" means trying something they
have not done before. The unknown may cause apprehension or even
fear in children. Activities may include going to an unknown place, eating new foods, learning a new skill, or finding out answers to the question of "Why?" This apprehension or fear may be alleviated by experiencing the activity or event step-by-step and side-by-side with an adult.

Left-brained children relate to the logical, sequential step process, and
they will draw conclusions by "looking at the differences." Right-brained
children will "look at the similarities" and enjoy the physical movement
required in many experiments. These right-brained children may flit
from one task to the next, but they will come to realize that in some
instances, one step may have to come before another may take place.
Both learning styles are conducive to this type of learning.

Informally, many parents expose children to the investigative process
when trying to answer the "Why?" questions. The first formal initiation
that children experience with this concept is in the elementary school
setting when teachers teach the process for science fair projects. Many
schools require all elementary students, even kindergartners, to complete
a project. Other schools make it a requirement for grades four through six
but elective for the primary grades. The educators understand that all

60   *Chapter 6*

children are not budding scientists, but the process involved is a key to learning. One of the science skills in the kindergarten curriculum is that of learning about the five senses: sight, smell, taste, hearing, and touch.

One girl at an elementary school chose this as her project and learned what the senses are and how each one helped her to keep safe and healthy. She also enjoyed it. She used the tops of five egg cartons and labeled each one with a card stating one of the five senses. Then she gathered many articles from around her house depicting that sense. In the one labeled "taste" she put a candy bar. By the time the judges came to review her project the candy bar was just the wrapper. When questioned by the judges, she responded, "You took so long that I got hungry."

The format for kindergarten through third grade is basic. Once this process is learned, the format may be augmented and expanded by adding additional steps and including more detail to the information. The five basic steps are:

1. Question: What is the problem or issue the children are trying to solve?
2. Hypothesis: What do children expect to happen in the experiment? (What are their guesses as to the outcome?)
3. Experiment: What is the procedure (the steps) they will use to discover the answer to their question?
4. Results: What is the data or the facts the children collected from the experiment?
5. Conclusion: What did the children learn from the experiment and what do these results mean?

For school science fair projects, the entire process is exhibited on a three-sided display board. It may contain pictures of the experiment, or the actual project may be in front of the board. Type "science fair projects" into your search bar and several sites will be available that depict the projects and display boards.

There is no "right" way or "wrong" way to carry out the investigative process. As with learning styles, there are "different" ways. Albert Einstein's style was visionary (right-brained), which led him to the process of exploring. Thomas Edison preferred to experiment (left-brained). Both men used the skills of logic, critical thinking, problem solving, and investigating, which, in some form or other, were instrumental in their accomplishments. Success in this process is obtained by learning from one's mistakes and then moving in a different direction, but nevertheless moving forward.

The most frustrating step of this process is selecting what the actual project will be. A very helpful website that will take away these frustrations was developed by the Akron Summit Public Library for information about science fair projects. After bringing up the site, type in "science fair projects" at the lower left side of the screen. The site is www.ascpl.lib.oh. us/.

There are three ways to search for your information on the Internet. These sources index everything on the Internet.

1. www.google.com
2. www.yahoo.com
3. Bing is also another source.

The following are sites that list the information by subject. They are smaller, but the information has been checked for relevance.

1. Librarians' Index to the Internet
2. www.VirtualLibrary.com

In the Home

When young children want something, they usually want it "right now!" They have not yet developed the concept of time. For example, at mealtime children may become very impatient and ask, "Why does it take so long?" This is the teaching moment, and a simplified version of the experimenting process may answer their question. The lunch menu will be tomato soup and crackers. First, show the children the clock, paying particular attention to the minute hand. They may not yet have learned to tell time, but they can learn that, as the big (minute) hand moves, time passes. Also expose children to digital clocks, as they will come into contact with both forms. This is the scenario for the experiment:

Question: Why does it take so long to get lunch ready?
(Show the child the directions on the can or package for preparing the soup. Read each step and explain, if necessary.)
Hypothesis: What do the children think will happen if they do as the directions indicate?
(The soup will be ready to eat.)
Experiment: What is the procedure?
(Open the can, put the contents in a bowl, and ask, "Is it ready yet?")
(Follow each directive step-by-step, asking after each step, "Is it ready yet?")
Results: What facts did the children collect from the experiment?
(All of these steps had to happen: open the can, put the contents in a soup bowl, add water or milk, stir, cover, put into microwave, set timer, wait. Get the crackers and pour milk into a glass. Look at the hands on the clock or the numbers on a digital clock and discuss how far they have moved since the experiment started. Avoid using the clock on the microwave, for young children may become

62   Chapter 6

confused when watching the numbers go in reverse order on the
timer.)

Conclusion: What did the children learn?

(By participating in the process, they learned what was required for a
meal to be prepared.

Try the same experiment with other projects or events that answer the
children's question of "Why does it take so long?" There will be times
when a trip to the library or the Internet will be needed to gather information for the project.

For example, children seem fascinated with magnets of all types (this
is a favorite science fair project.) It may be accomplished by both left-
brained and right-brained children and still result in the same conclusion.
Left-brained: The first step (the parts) in the logical sequence of the research is to use books or the Internet to find out what a magnet is and
why it works as it does. Next, give the children an assortment of magnets
and allow them to go all around the house and try to pick up items with
the magnet. (This is their favorite part.) As they do that, follow along and
keep two lists, one of items the magnet picks up and the other of items it
does not.

Right-brained: These children see the whole picture first; that is, magnets pick up some objects and not others. Do the same activity. Give the
child the magnets and keep the list. Then research why the magnet
picked up some items and did not pick up others (the whole picture
dictates what parts are needed).

In the World

"There has to be a better way!" Children experience many situations
in which they believe this to be true. They have many responses of "Why
can't you . . . ?" This is the time to let them experiment and invent, with
supervision, of course. In a fourth-grade class the students were required
to create and invent something that would improve their life.

One boy recently had had a visit to the dentist for a teeth cleaning. As
usual, he complained about the bright light above his head. He knew
what he wanted to invent. He decided that if the dentist had a minuscule
light attached to the cleaning tool, he could see inside the mouth and
would not need the overhead light. Easier said than done.

His mom took him all over town (a large city) trying to find a light
small enough. The smallest he could find was like the one his mom had
attached to her key ring. So he bought that one for his experiment. His
dentist was enthralled with his idea and gave him some old cleaning
tools he no longer used. The boy worked hard to construct the device.
When finished, he experimented on himself and realized the device was

too cumbersome for comfort. But, like Edison, he did not fail. He simply found one way that did not work.

The boy had also researched the Internet for dentist supplies but did not find anything similar to what he had in mind. When researching the project, remember the rules for what makes the information valid:

What is the source? Is it credible? (Is it someone's opinion or proven facts?)

Is the information up-to-date? (Some of the early teacher training methods would not be relevant for the high-tech world of today.)

Is the information objective? (Does the source have a stake in selling you their product, or are they giving you factual information?)

Does the information come from at least three sources?

In School

Experimenting is not just for science. It is used in every area of the curriculum.

Mathematics: Some students first learn the term "hypothesis" in their high school geometry math class. Mathematicians and economists deal with the concept and process daily.

Writing and social studies: The science fair project includes a written report of the process from inception to completion. Every author, no matter what type of writing, follows the same scenario:

- Question or purpose: Why am I writing this?
- Hypotheses: When I finish, what message do I want understood by the reader?
- Experiment: Where do I research the data, and what information will I use?
- Result: What facts did I learn and want my readers to learn?
- Conclusion: How did this information help both the writer and the reader?

An important aspect of every experiment is the checking and double-checking of all information. In writing it is called editing; vocabulary may be changed, sequence of sentences or even paragraphs may be shifted, data may be added or eliminated, and format may be altered. Every experimenter rechecks the facts and details before considering the project completed.

In other areas of the curriculum the project may be an experiment to create a better form of wheat, a hybrid form of fruit or vegetable that is healthier for humans, or a product that is safer than insecticides. Equipment may be experimented with to become more effective and efficient. Experimenters also research the cultures of the past in order to improve

64   *Chapter 6*

life in the future. To experiment means to not simply accept "what is" but to try to create "what is a better way."

In the Home

A favorite question, beginning with the four-year-old and continuing through early childhood, is "Why?" Your first response is "Let's find out." The process may be a simple one found in a book or on the Internet. But the process may also be more complex and lend itself toward investigating and then experimenting.

For example, the question might be, "Where does the snow go when it goes away?" The investigation shows what causes snow, what the composition is, and the role weather has in its coming and going. The young child will listen to the explanation, see some pictures in a book, or see an article on the Internet. But now go a step further and "show" the child what happens. Use four plastic food containers or four foam cups for your experiment. Fill each about half with fresh snow (southerners may do a similar experiment with rain water). Put one in the freezer, one in the refrigerator, and one on the kitchen counter, and leave one outside. Make a chart to record findings.

Teach the correct vocabulary. Primary age children can learn "consistency" in this context, for the word has meaning. They may even be able to read it "con-sis-ten-cy." Another word is "constant," as in, "the freezer temperature remains constant." Maintain the chart for a few days, allowing the children to discover what happens.

Table 6.1. Where Does Snow Go?

Place	Time	Temperature	Consistency
Freezer (at factory setting)	8:00 a.m.	0 degrees	soft
	noon	0 degrees	hard/frozen
	6:00 p.m.	0 degrees	frozen
Refrigerator			Follow the same pattern: the factory setting for refrigerators is 37 degrees.
Counter			Follow the same pattern: record the temperature in your home.
Outdoors			Follow the same pattern: recording the temperature outdoors; this will vary. For outdoors, use a thermometer or check the Internet for your area.

In the World

This is your opportunity to teach the child the value of money. The child will need pencils for school. Go to an office supply store, a large discount store, a grocery store, and a gas station/food mart. Check the type of pencil the boy wants. Then record the cost at each store.

Back at home, tell him that he has a specific amount of money and ask where he would like to buy his pencils. Tell him that he will need a dozen pencils so he has some in reserve. Then help him (or have an older sibling do the math) compute how much he would have to pay in each store for the same item. Use the diagrams in chapter 5 for this project. This is a time-consuming experiment, but a good lesson. The next time it will not take as long.

At School

Experimenting is used in every area of the elementary curriculum. This is the skill that is hands-on and teaches the "how," "why," or "is there a better way?"

Science: The study of living things, their needs, and their interaction with their environment is an important segment of the science curriculum in the primary grades. The students become involved in the study of plants, with the curriculum in each grade level becoming more complex and detailed. The experiments begin in kindergarten and first grade with each child planting a vegetable or flower seed in a foam cup or similar container. The theme revolves around the need for water and sunlight. The following is a typical class project:

- One plant is put into the closet and ignored.
- The second plant is put on the window sill and ignored.
- The third plant is put in a dark area with no sunlight and given water as needed.
- The fourth plant is put on the window sill and given water as needed.

A log is kept as to the progress of each.

Reading/writing: Experimenting in the writing process has already been discussed. Many times, a story in the reading textbook will revolve around a concept taught in science. One story in the second-grade book was a mystery and included children writing a note with "invisible ink." The students were enthralled, trying several experiments using different substances to see what would and would not work. The recipe for this experiment is explained and listed in chapter 12. It is easy for children to do, fun, and very informative.

Math: Math involves the process of experimenting using mathematical terms and concepts. The bulletin board in one second-grade classroom in

66   *Chapter 6*

October contained pictures of objects and scenes for Halloween and was used for teaching vowel sounds. For example, a bat was used for the "short a" sound and a spider for the "long I" sound. Both bats and spiders were studied in the science lessons.

These students were given a sheet of black construction paper to use in making a bat similar to the one on the bulletin board. At second grade some patterns are still used for tracing the craft item, also using eye-hand coordination and fine motor skills. The children were given a pattern that was half the picture of the bat. They discussed several options, and as each child suggested an idea, it was tried. They learned many ways that did not work. The options were:

- Borrow a pattern from another student, place them together, and trace.
- Trace two, cut them out, and tape them together.
- Fold the paper, put the pattern in the middle of the paper, trace the pattern, and cut it out.
- Fold the pattern, place it on the edge (not the fold) of the paper, trace it, and cut it out.
- Finally, many children realized that if they placed the straight side of the pattern on the fold, it would work. It did.

The other lesson, following a similar format, was making the spider. This is explained in chapter 12.

Social Studies: A major part of social studies in elementary school is geography. This encompasses weather and temperature that dictate how and where people live. One story, a favorite of second-graders, was *Curious George Flies a Kite*. Each child made a small kite of construction paper, and they tried flying them in several situations:

- Outdoors on a calm day
- In the classroom
- Running around the gymnasium creating wind
- Outdoors on a rainy day (A parent was helping, and she put on rain gear, went outdoors by the classroom window, and ran with her kite.)
- Outdoors on a windy day. The children participated with their own kite. A discussion followed on how these weather conditions (wind, rain, snow, cold, and heat) impacted plants, animals, and how people live.

All of these lessons are projects that span a few to several days, and one lesson builds on another. In many of the projects, the students work in small teams. This is also part of the curriculum of learning to work together socially and share the workload.

The Digging In

SEVEN

A Child's "Work" Is "Play"

Children play through necessity, not just to have fun. Children are responding to the developmental needs of their bodies.

There are four fields of human behavior, all of which develop sequentially from birth. These are motor (physical movement and agility), adaptive (the body adjusting to its environment), language (words and sounds), and personal-social (relationships and reaction to others). Nature takes care that the basic instincts are fulfilled; thus, children's initial learning takes place through play. The adult does not have to teach the children how to play; it comes naturally. Be aware that too much "organized play" may be detrimental.

Play is essential for growth. In the age of technology, it is even more essential. None of the four fields of development are developed through moving fingers and thumb on a computer or handheld device. Consider the teenage girl who set a record for the most text messages sent in one month, and that girl was proud of herself. She is limiting her natural growth and development. The skills required to use and understand technology are vital, but it is just as vital to give equal time to the rest of the world.

Play is needed to promote and advance the five skills. Take your clues from the children as to how much they can handle and when they can handle it. Of course, there will be times when they need some adult motivation or a little push (not a shove) of encouragement.

Through this play, creativity emerges and blooms. The selection of activities follows a sequence for the children. The first learning takes place through the sandbox, water table, dirt and mud (really!), dolls and stuffed animals, cars, trucks, airplanes, wagons, tricycles, and dramatic play (house, school, hospital, astronauts). At the right time for the children the learning takes a more academic aspect.

70   *Chapter 7*

Even within one activity, age dictates the quality and quantity of the progress. Children like to build, creating a variety of structures.

- The four-year-olds, the age of large muscle activity, enjoy big blocks. They will build a tower, which they call a building. They will also arrange the blocks end-to-end on the floor to see how far they will go.
- The five- to six-year-olds prefer smaller blocks and build roads and tunnels for their trucks and cars. Some girls may build simple structures for their dolls.
- The six- to seven-year-olds move on to yet smaller blocks and Lego-type building materials. The creations are far more detailed. Some children tend toward building vehicles and structures dealing with transportation, while others build structures for their dramatic play (schools, hospitals, houses).
- The seven- to eight-year-olds take the project to a higher level. They will use any materials at their disposal to be very creative. Materials may be boxes of all sizes, a variety of building blocks, Popsicle sticks, string, rubber bands or wire, fabric, and whatever other materials they find around the house. Of course, they will need glue and tape.[1]

The primary criterion for the selection of play materials is the age of the child. Cultural and gender differences and intelligence play a minor role in this decision.

Children develop from head to toe and from the center of the body outward. The large motor skills (arms and legs) need to be developed before small motor skills (hands and fingers). Every day should include some type of physical activity: playground equipment (backyard, school, or park), bike riding, jump rope, or playing with large trucks. For those living in apartments and cities, the choices are sometimes limited. One option might be to use an aerobic DVD as a fun workout. Perfection in following what is on the screen is not important; movement is the key.

A kindergarten boy lived in an apartment building with limited facilities and inside space. His grandmother sent him a creative birthday gift. Materials needed: a piece of denim (one yard by about four feet), blue electrical tape, a variety of small vehicles (Matchbox size), a set of small building blocks, and a canvas tote bag for easy storage. The fabric was spread on the floor and the tape was put on it to make roads (as a roadmap of a small city). These materials, his city, stored neatly in the tote bag. He and his dad spent hours playing, on the floor in the living room or bedroom. The five-year-old used many muscles crawling around on the floor when "operating" the vehicles around his city.

Doing household chores is also a great way to develop motor skills. For large muscles: make a bed, put clothes on hangers, sweep the floor, vacuum carpets, dust furniture (children like the feather dusters), set the table, and load the dishwasher (small children can load the silverware). For small muscles: match and fold socks, fold washcloths and small towels, fold underwear or other clothing that goes into a drawer, and pick up small toys.

MOTOR DEVELOPMENT

The development from large to small motor coordination follows an exact sequence, but the time line may vary. By adulthood, it is not important whether children walked at one year old or two years old, or whether the children wrote their name at four years old or six years old. The task was accomplished in the order that was right for each child. Some adults become upset if the children are not yet ready for developmental tasks on the parent's time line. Think of it this way: adults understand that children's teeth come in when development dictates, and there is absolutely nothing anyone can do to speed up the process. The same premise is true for the rest of the development of children. The following are general guidelines, not absolutes:

- Four years old: This is the "expansive" age. The children run, jump, climb, gallop, swing, and do somersaults. They need outside play, particularly on equipment. They begin to manage large buttons, string large wooden or plastic beads, and some may manage scissors. Start with blunt-end scissors. Then use clay and roll out a long piece that looks like a snake. Practice cutting this into pieces. It is soft, pliant, and easy in learning how to use a scissors.
- Five years old: The children are still active but change the activity often. They still prefer large motor activities. The kindergarten teacher schedules activities for a short duration and alternates physical activities with more sedate ones. These children like freedom of movement (select clothes accordingly), will change position often, but will continue working. They need an outdoor space inside the classroom or the house. A baby bathtub becomes a mini sandbox or a water tub filled with rubber animals and boats for play. Large blocks and easels also use large muscles. For writing, use materials that mark easily (markers or paintbrushes) and use large pencils made for the small hands.
- Six years old: The children will continually move while working: kneeling on the chair and leaning over the desk; sitting in the regular position; standing with both feet on the floor and leaning over the desk, or putting one foot on the floor with the other knee on the chair while leaning over the desk. But they do not disturb anyone else, and assignments are completed. A first-grade teacher used child-size rocking chairs for the reading group. A few children would rock with such vigor that the teacher told them she thought

72   *Chapter 7*

they were going to take off. This brought forth a "VROOM! VROOM!" which delighted the class. Movement helped the focus.

- Seven years old: These children go to extremes with their movement. They may be very physically active one minute and then quiet and still the next. Popular activities are climbing trees, bicycling, jumping rope, or playing ball. The fine motor skill has developed so they can catch the ball with their hands, not with their arms and body. They will grasp the pencil tightly and then stop, for their hands get tired.
- Children are not fully ready for manuscript writing until about nine years old.

EYE ORIENTATION AND EYE-HAND COORDINATION

There are two issues of importance that dictate success for children in school activities. This is based on age, not intelligence.

The first is eye orientation. This comes into play with the back-and-forth eye movement from desk to the board (age eight); from a textbook to the paper on the desk (age seven to eight); and from reading to the end of a line, moving down and to the left to begin the next line (age seven). In first and second grades, the math textbook is in a workbook form and the children write directly in the book. By third grade, the text is a hardcover and not to be written in, thus requiring children to look in the book, copy the math problems on their paper, and then work the problems.

Some first- and second-graders use their finger to follow along with each word as they read. Others put a bookmark under the line, read the line, move the bookmark down, and continue. These activities help children orient their eyes to the reading material. It is okay. They will discontinue the process when they are ready.

The second skill is that of eye-hand coordination, that is, commanding the hands and fingers to do what the eyes want them to do. For the four-year-old, it is eye-arm coordination. Watch children try to catch a ball as they use their arms to trap it and bring it into their bodies. They have the concept, and they catch the ball in the manner of a natural large-motor four-year-old.

Handedness, right or left, is established in the five-year-old. They write or draw more comfortably with objects that are easy to hold and make a mark without much pressure. Markers and paintbrushes are the tool of choice. If pencils are used, rubber grips are available to allow the children a firmer hold. By six, children are still awkward when trying to write, but they like these activities. They make the letters and numbers large; thus, the paper used has the lines about ¾ to 1 inch apart. By third grade they are ready for regular lined notebook paper. Reversing letters

A Child's "Work" Is "Play"

and numbers is common for some children through ages six-and-a-half and seven.

The seven-year-old is the eraser king. They grip the pencil so tightly that their fingers get tired and mistakes are made. They also may reverse letters and numbers, but they recognize the mistake when it is made; hence, the eraser. Their inability to copy from the board is not just one of orientation; their eyes do not shift readily from near to far.

By eight, third grade, the process seems to have developed to their comfort level. Some children who have been thought to have had a reading problem were simply trying to accomplish activities that their body was not yet developed sufficiently to handle.

Again, take your cue from the children. They will readily do tasks within their stage of development. Help them find ways of accomplishing these tasks within their capabilities. *Note:* With technology, handwriting is used less and a printer is used more. But the skill must still be learned. Remember, the activities they select as their choice for play will advance these skills.

NOTE

1. Gesell, Arnold, Frances I. Ilg, and Louise Bates Ames. *The Child from Five to Ten.* New York: Harper & Row Publishers, revised 1977.

EIGHT

Logic

TECHNIQUES, STRATEGIES, AND ACTIVITIES

This collection of techniques, strategies, and activities, chapters 8 through 12, are for reading and storing away for the opportune time for teaching the skill. Be creative. Use what is written here as the catalyst to other ideas that are more apropos to your children and your situation.

1.) Sequence: Cooking activities are instrumental to teaching the skill of sequencing; that is, one step has to come before another. At the beginning of the project, discuss the sequence of creating the meal, even if it is just fixing a sandwich or cereal for breakfast. Start with simple creations that will contain as few steps as possible. This will become the child's own recipe file.

Use index cards, larger ones for younger children, and store them in any sort of box, decorated and labeled by the child. Older children may transfer the file to their computer or handheld device. It is most convenient for the children to have their recipes on file readily available in the kitchen. This activity is for both boys and girls. Each one will experience a time when they have to prepare their own meal, even if it is just a sandwich, soup, frozen dinner, or frozen pizza.

2.) Sequence: Making brownies from a boxed mix is an activity that teaches sequence, reading, vocabulary, and life skills. Start with the box and a highlighter. Highlight the important steps in the process. Then allow the children to do as much of the work as they can handle, by following the steps exactly. This activity may easily transfer to other cooking projects.

3.) Sequence: At the end of the day (periodically, not every day) list the activities that happened that day. Discuss how a particular event had to happen before the next one took place. Allow the right-brained children to list what they remember in any order. Make the list in the order that it is dictated. Then go back and number the lists in order as they happened, so the children develop a sense of a step-by-step process.

4.) Sequence: Make a time line of a school project or event. For example, when planning a birthday party, first list the "to-dos" that must lead up to the event: buy invitations, write and send invitations, buy decorations and favors, plan where it will be held, plan the menu, plan activities, plan shopping for needed items, plan who does what.

Next, number them in the order in which they must be accomplished. On a printed calendar, write when each task will be done and post it for all to see. Use this same process when the children are assigned a school project, a book report, an essay, or a science fair project. This is a reminder to those who wait until the last minute to do the work and then find that they have run out of time.

5.) Sequence: Are we there yet? Set up a system for the children to follow while traveling that will keep them occupied. This activity could be a task that keeps the children informed as to where they are at all times and how much farther it is to the destination.

Provide the child with a map which includes both a picture of the route and a written scenario. This map may be a paper commercial version or a printout from the computer that allows the children to visualize the route from start to finish and to highlight as they travel. Having the paper version puts something in their hands, keeps them occupied with the task, and teaches them how to read a map. If the children are using public transportation, make a list of the stops they will pass before their destination. If the trip is by air, keep a watch available and provide plenty of activities. They still may get impatient and fidgety, but knowing the step-by-step process will help them deal with the situation.

6.) Sequence: Picture documentation of event: Take pictures of a school field trip, family event, or a vacation. Print them out, either on glossy paper or regular computer paper. Allow the children to arrange them in order as they happened. If it was a special event for the children and they want to save the memories, put them into an individual photo album or a homemade paper scrapbook. To make it even more memorable, write a sentence or two about each picture, including names, to add to the book.

7.) Cause/Effect: For elementary school children, doing homework and handing it in to the teacher are two entirely different tasks. The left-brained children complete it, put it into their backpack for school, and then follow the classroom rules for where and when to turn it in. The right-brained children will complete the assignment and believe that is the end of the process. They may leave it where they did it, put it into their backpack for school, or put it into their desk if it is done at school. But somehow it does not seem to get to the teacher.

A follow-through system (short term of no more than a few weeks) needs to be set up between teacher, parent, and child until that child becomes accustomed to the process and realizes that the grade depends on the teacher receiving the finished work. This may be done in one of two ways.

Before computers, teachers have asked the parent to purchase a small (3-inch by 5-inch). spiral notebook. Teachers are busy at the end of the school day, so the parent would make a list of the subject areas on the page. The teacher just checked the areas in which the children had homework that night and added a signature. The parent would ask the children for the notebook each day when they arrived home from school. After the homework was finished, the parent checked it, signed the bottom of that day's page, and watched the children put it into their backpack. If the book did not get home or to school, there were preset consequences.

The parent of a first-grade boy was advised to set up this system. It worked and resulted in higher report card grades. But the boy was not happy with it and said, "Why did my teacher have to think of this?" In this technological age, the second option would be to set up a similar system through e-mails or on the child's handheld device.

8.) Cause/Effect: Every cause has some sort of effect, some positive and some negative. Understanding what "effects" are and witnessing what they may look like helps the children put more thought into their actions and the results of those actions.

Be a people watcher when you are at the mall or in a restaurant or at an event. Indicate a person who is displaying some emotion, happy or sad. Ask the children, "What do you think happened to make the person look like that?" Of course, not knowing the truth, the children will guess all sorts of scenarios. The children will use experiences from their own life that would have elicited that response.

Briefly state the fact that everything a person does will have a response, and that person needs to consider what that might be before they act. State that this includes children as well as adults. Sometimes a person needs to think of the hoped-for response and act accordingly. For example, if the children want to make the honor roll, they need to do all their homework and class work assignments. These discussions are not planned in advance; they happen when the occasion dictates a dialogue.

78   *Chapter 8*

9.) Cause/Effect: An event or activity is a prime time to discuss possible effects and give the children information to ponder when making a decision. Example: The children want to begin an activity such as join an athletic team or scouts, or take music lessons. On paper or the computer, draw a large letter *T*. At the top left place a big minus sign and at the top right draw a plus sign. Think of every type of effect that might result from engaging in the activity and write it in the proper column. Chapter 5 has formats that are conducive to this activity, thus combining the skills of logic and investigating.

This activity also may be used to help alleviate fears when the children are going to be exposed to new experiences. Moving to a new town or new part of the same town and going to a new school cause the children to be very apprehensive. This activity, especially the positive results that may arise from the move, contributes to helping the children accept the situation with less fear and more interest.

10.) Summary: Recap a movie, book, or activity. After experiencing one of these activities, ask the children to write a brief summary of what they experienced. Require this activity to be accomplished before they text or call a friend to discuss the event (see chapter 2). The children may balk at doing "schoolwork" before sharing the information. Indicate that the friend wants to enjoy the story of what happened, so the telling of it must include the best parts and have a beginning, middle, and end, not an end, a beginning, and a middle, or just that child's favorite parts.

11.) Summary: Writing a petition. When the children complain of an unfair or unpleasant situation, use the opportunity to teach the children a positive method to use in trying to right the situation. First, summarize the issues that the children think should be changed. This may be done in the form of a list. Then for each item, state what the children feel would be a better solution. The children might involve others in their classroom or team or troop who feel the same way. After it is put in writing, each child will sign it.

Remember, this is a positive exercise, and each issue is stated as a fact, not a complaint. The next step is to take it to the person who has the authority to make the changes, the teacher, the school principal, the coach, or the leader. Success is achieved if the person in charge listens to the children and especially if some of the issues are changed for the better.

12.) Summary: Create a log of the books read by the children. Many public libraries conduct summer programs that award prizes for a set number of books read over the two-month period. Set up a system that lists and summarizes each book read. Include title, author, characters, setting, plot (in a few sentences), and conclusion (if the book has one).

Logic   79

This may be set up as a list, or you may prefer to use one of the book report formats listed at the end of this chapter.

Many schools also require reading a few books during the summer vacation, selected from the list provided by the teacher. At the beginning of the next school year, book reports are to be turned in to the new teacher. This activity will make the task easier for the children as they have already documented the information in their log.

13.) Summary: Illustrate the story. For younger children, after reading a picture story, create a "book." Use computer paper and fold it in half so there are now four pages, five-and-a-half by eight-and-a-half. Print the title and author on the first page, leaving room for a drawing. On each of the other three pages, print a sentence, dictated by the children, of an event in the book. The children will then illustrate their book. This is a fun rainy day or summer activity.

14.) Predictions: What will the story be about? At the library, in the book store, or on a book site on the Internet, read titles with the children, look at the cover of the book, and then predict what the book might be about. Next, look for the summary that might be written on the back cover, on a separate page in the front of the book, or, if you are online, read the summary provided by the publisher. This activity helps the children decide if they think it will be a story that will interest them. If they just decided by the picture on the cover, they may be disappointed, as the book may turn out to be much different than they had originally thought.

15.) Predictions: Options for handling situations. After children have acted inappropriately in a situation, discuss other actions that may have been a better solution to the problem. For each option, predict what may have been the result if that had been their choice. Consider at least three other choices they may have used. This activity leads to using better judgment in future situations.

16.) Book report format.

Title:_____

Author:_____

Who (Main Character):_____

(Character Traits)_____

Who (Second Character)_____

(Character Traits)_____

Where (Setting):_____

What (Problem or Goal):_____

_____

How Solved:_____

_____

Why (Optional-Author's purpose for the book or lesson learned):_____

_____

80   *Chapter 8*

17.) Book report format:

Title
_____

Author
_____

Characters (Who)
_____   _____

Character Traits
_____   _____

_____   _____

Setting (Where)
_____

Plot (What)
Problem/Goal:_____

_____

Solution:_____

_____

Purpose (Why - Optional)
What was the Author's purpose or the lesson learned:_____

_____

_____

NINE

Critical Thinking

TECHNIQUES, STRATEGIES, AND ACTIVITIES

1.) Key Words and Phrases: Make an ongoing chart that helps the children define and explain "key words and phrases."

What a key opens (item)	What a key unlocks (information)
Door	Map
Padlock	Mystery story
Car	Math signs
Luggage	Scientific procedure
Safe	Spelling rules

2.) Key Words and Phrases: Create a running list of words and phrases that are keys to information. Example: Math: more than, less than, in all, all together, how many for each . . . , how many times. Sequence: before, after, next, first, last, finally, middle. Space: above, below, over, under, next to, beside.

3.) Key Words and Phrases: Play "Simon Says." Listen for key words before moving. First, don't do a thing unless "Simon Says." Next, listen for exact numbers and movement directions.

4.) Key Words and Phrases: Read a mystery story. List the words that are keys to solving the mystery.

5.) Key Words and Phrases: Use a road map (old-fashioned paper one, atlas, computer generated) and read the key to compute distances, locate hospitals and schools, and identify roads (two-lane, four-lane, and interstate), rivers, and railroads.

81

82   *Chapter 9*

6.) Key Words and Phrases: In newspapers, magazines, and mail-delivered ads highlight the words that are keys to selling the product.

7.) Key Words and Phrases: Teach a lesson on paper folding, origami. Libraries and the Internet have books and activities for children that explain the process. Note the key words for each step.

8.) Key Words and Phrases: Prepare a scavenger hunt. This is a fun activity for a child's party. Make the lists short and give exact directions as to what houses are acceptable sources. Check with neighbors first. This can also be done at school, but the staff needs to be notified in advance and sources need to be preapproved.

9.) Key Words and Phrases: After reading a story in a book, magazine, or reading or social studies textbook, either highlight (color code to differentiate meaning) or make a list (depending on whether or not the document may be written in) of key words that designate meaning. Example: fact/fiction, reality/fantasy, likenesses/differences, beginning/middle/end, or true/false.

10.) Key Words and Phrases: Build a structure or vehicle from wooden blocks, Popsicle sticks, plastic blocks, clay (recipe at end of this chapter), fabric, or other "stuff." The child will follow written or oral directions to complete the task. Before starting, the children will identify the key words that specify the step-by-step process.

11.) Main Idea: Set up the scenario of a situation (main idea) that may very possibly happen in the children's life. This may be at school, on their Little League team, in scouting, or in general day-to-day activities. Examples are another child shoving to the front of a line, a name-calling bully, another child tripping or pushing your child, handling accusations that are false, or a menacing bully.

These examples are the main idea, or jist, of the situation. Now discuss several options the children might use to handle or defuse the situation. You are sending the children out into the world with techniques and strategies to protect themselves. The children may not think the solution at the time is "fair," but they will learn when to persist and when to walk away.

12.) Main Idea: Make a chart for a selection from a story (reading or social studies) that will help the children in drawing conclusions and comprehending the information. Example:

Details from the text   What is implied   Conclusion

13.) Main Idea: Select a topic for a story. The teacher may assign a general topic for a story, such as, "Write a story about your summer vacation." Use the format in chapter 3 to brainstorm options for the topic. Then use the same format to brainstorm all the points to use in the story that tell about the particular event in question. This has two parts. First, the children select the main idea for the story, possibly "going to camp."

Then the children select the main idea that tells why the camp was so important, possibly "learning to paddle a canoe."

14.) Main Idea: This activity is for the younger children. Show the children the cover of a magazine or a book that they haven't read. Have them draw a picture of what they think the story is about. This picture may have two or three parts.

15.) Main Idea/Purpose: In a newspaper, compare and contrast articles into categories: news, features, or editorials. The type of article dictates its purpose. Compile lists that identify each category:

News article: Facts, sources listed, quotes, data, details
Feature article: descriptions, some opinions, appeals to emotions, memorable events, some facts
Editorial: opinions, some facts or data cited, written to influence

16.) Main Idea: Write a list of story titles in the left-hand column. Then write a sentence that may be the main idea of the book in the right-hand column, but not in the same chronological order. The child has the task of matching each title with the sentence that would be a logical main idea.

17.) Key Words/Purpose: Introduce the children to advertising words that "sell." Use the ads that come in the mail or are in newspapers, magazines, or websites. Highlight the words that are there to influence the reader to want to buy the product. Some key words will make the product appeal to the buyer, but other key words will make the buyer want to buy, such as *sale, half price, two-for-one, only ___ left, last day to buy, new and improved*, or *the best offer available*.

18.) Key Words/Purpose: Take the children grocery shopping. Allow enough time, for this trip will take longer than usual. Stress nutrition and price. Teach the key words to look for on the box or package: first look for serving size, then read the calories, fat, carbohydrates, sugar, and sodium. Cereals are an interesting section in which to start. Example: one cereal that boasted "most fiber," but as the children read the rest of the information, they saw that the sugar content was very high. Then compare brands by ingredients and price.

19.) Recipe for modeling clay: This recipe has been used in schools for many years; the source is unknown. Store it in tight containers (margarine containers are great) and use plastic place mats when working. This also may be used to teach letter formation and develop fine motor coordination. Roll it like a snake and then break off pieces to make either the stick or round letters. The plus is that it can be reused.

Ingredients

1 cup flour
1 cup water
2 teaspoons cream of tartar (DO NOT OMIT)

84   *Chapter 9*

1 tablespoon cooking oil
½ cup salt
Food coloring

Stress to children that this mixture is not for eating.

In a heavy aluminum saucepan, mix the dry ingredients. Add the oil, water, and food coloring. Cook 3 minutes on medium heat or until the mixture pulls away from the sides of the pan. Knead slightly, almost immediately. Store in an airtight container.

TEN

Problem Solving

TECHNIQUES, STRATEGIES, AND ACTIVITIES

1.) Drawing Conclusions: Take a walk with your children in your yard, down the street, in the park, or on the beach. Bring along some sort of tote bag. This adventure is to collect objects of a specific genre: rocks, seashells, or leaves. The second part of the activity takes place when you return home. Tell the children to arrange the items in any order they would like. Then ask them to see how many other ways they can arrange them; for example, by size, shape, color, texture, or other detail.

They will draw conclusions as to the attributes of specific items as well as develop vocabulary of descriptive words, such as big/little, smooth/rough, colorful/drab, round/oval/free shape. In addition they will learn the meanings of verbs and nouns, such as sort, categorize, arrange, compare/contrast, likenesses/differences, and uses/purposes. Compliment them on their creativity. Remember, left-brained children look for differences and right-brained children look for the similarities.

2.) Drawing Conclusions: Follow the format for the activity in #1, but instead of collecting items in a specific category, add more categories to increase the skill level. Examples might be items made of wood (pencils, ruler, picture frame), metal (silverware, stapler, kettle), paper (envelope, notebook paper, magazine). Categorize them by uses, feel, shape, color, or size. The children may select another very creative way in which to sort the items. They have to draw conclusions as to the attributes of the items in order to accomplish this task. It also teaches them to look for the details, not just an overview.

3.) Drawing Conclusions: Play the age-old game of "Twenty Questions." As the game progresses, the children will draw conclusions as to the use or category of the answer. This skill is also useful in investigating

86   *Chapter 10*

and experimenting. The children have to put information together to come to a conclusion. This is the premise of the book; don't tell them the answer, guide them in the process of finding the answer themselves.

4.) Drawing Conclusions: This activity is both enlightening and fun. Collect some objects from grandma's house: a manual can opener, a wire basket for popping corn, a wind-up wall pencil sharpener, or a metal hand ice-cube tray. Another site to observe this type of item is a store that sells camping supplies. The children examine the item and from the attributes, guess the purpose of it (probably over much awe and laughter).

5.) Drawing Conclusions: For even older objects that are not as easily identifiable, visit your historical society. A small rural town recently opened a new site. A teacher took her class on a field trip to learn the history of that town. One object they saw mystified them. It was a long handle (like a broom), and the bottom resembled a comb, except the "teeth" of this comb were made of sharp metal. It was a lawn mower from the eighteen hundreds! Not one child or even the teacher was able to identify what it was used for. In addition to teaching the children to look for details to draw the conclusion as to the use, it was a history lesson.

6.) Drawing Conclusions: Create and read riddles. Children love them. This is especially fun for the eight-year-old whose sense of humor appreciates the logic and the puns. They may be found in children's magazines and books in the library. Some of the riddles really take creative thinking.

7.) Inferences: Recognizing what is missing. With young children (preschool and kindergarten) start with three items completely unrelated to each other (fork, pencil, and key). Allow the children to look at each one. Then block the child's sight from the objects as you remove one of them. Then tell the children to look at what is still there and ask them, "What is missing?" Repeat the activity several times using different objects. Increase the difficulty by adding more items, one at a time. Another way to increase the difficulty is to select items closer in relation to each other (knife, fork, teaspoon, and tablespoon) or to take away more than one item at a time.

8.) Inferences: Relating parts to the whole. Select a wooden puzzle, six to eight pieces. Block the child's view and take one piece away. The child shows where the missing piece was and states what was in the piece. Example: The puzzle is of a single dog. The piece taken away was one of the hind legs of the dog. The format is similar to that in #7. To increase the difficulty, use pictures with more than one item in them. The pictures may be the front of a cereal box or a picture of a magazine. Cut them into several pieces to make the puzzle. These cost no money and may be used several times and then tossed away in place of new pictures made into puzzles.

Problem Solving 87

9.) Inferences: What is missing? For older school-age children, make puzzles a common activity. These may be made found in children's magazines or puzzle books purchased at your local store. All five skills are involved. Vary the selection of puzzles: picture puzzles (made or purchased), logic, crossword, and sudoku (math). Some of the magazines have puzzles with two similar pictures in which the child finds several items that are different (example, the boy's shoes might be loafers in one picture and sneakers in the other). These magazines are good time fillers for restless children on car trips.

10.) Inferences: What is missing? Select a story (children's reading level) from a magazine, textbook, or library book. If the material may be written in, blacken out a sentence that contains information important to the comprehension of the story. If it is a textbook, copy the selection you are using for this purpose. Use a selection that is unfamiliar to the children. Read the selection. Ask the children for options of what material may be missing in order to fully understand the meaning or to come to a conclusion. Use several different paragraphs from a story, selecting a different piece of information each time you read it. Allow the children to follow the same procedure and have you guess what information was missing.

11.) Inferences: Categories and Classification. Depending on the age of the children, use actual items, then pictures, and finally words. Use four items to start, three in the same category, and the fourth one from another category; example: three animals and one flower. With this activity, you are asking the children to select "What does not belong?" To increase the difficulty, add items or narrow the category: for example, three dogs and one horse. *Note:* In the activities in which the children are looking for "what is missing," they are looking for details that are implied but not written. In this type of activity they hear all the information, but they have to discriminate between what is relevant and what is not.

12.) Inferences: What is missing? Cut some circle, square, rectangle, and triangle shapes (math concepts) from various colors of construction paper or from pieces of fabric. The instructions for this activity are to select a shape (or two) and paste it on a sheet of printing paper. Then decide what the finished product will be and, using crayons or markers, draw the rest of the picture. The children see what is there and draw what is inferred.

For a lesson with second-graders, one teacher gave each child a piece of brown fake fur in the shape of an oval (math and a lesson about bears) and a sheet of drawing paper. They could use crayons or markers. She told them to draw the rest of the picture. In another lesson using colored geometric shapes, the students became quite creative. They created wagons (rectangle and circles), houses (squares or rectangles), and even pyramids (triangles).

88   *Chapter 10*

13.) Inferences: Select the comic section of the newspaper or a cartoon in a child's magazine. These cartoons use the skill of inference for their humor. Discuss what is said, what is not said, or in some cases, the double meaning.

14.) Inferences: Read mystery books. Many are written for young children. As the story progresses, discuss what clues are stated and then ask the children what else they need to know in order to solve the mystery.

15.) Inferences: Often teachers or parents issue statements or commands that require the children to infer what is missing and act accordingly. When doing this, after the children follow through with what they are being asked or told to do, ask them what was missing from what the teacher or parent said. Many times what is inferred is the children's names or the words "class" or "students." For example:

- It is lunch time. Line up. (The children are to line up at the classroom door.)
- On the playground, the teacher raises her hand. (The children see it and know that recess is over and they are to line up. Not one word is said.)
- The teacher announces, "It is math time." (The students know that they must get their math books from inside their desks.)
- Mom knocks loudly on the bedroom door of each child and says, "Breakfast in fifteen minutes." (The children know to get up and dressed and to the table or they will miss breakfast.)
- "Here comes the school bus!" (The children know that the bus is coming and they had better hurry out to their school bus stop.)

ELEVEN

Investigating

TECHNIQUES, STRATEGIES, AND ACTIVITIES

1.) Compare/Contrast: Classification. Children are part of the family; thus, they should contribute to the welfare of that family. Young children are assigned the minor chores, which increase with age and maturity. However, these chores also contribute to the children's education. Classifying objects (size, shape, color, use), that is, identifying the details, is part of the investigative process. Some chores involve eye-hand coordination and fine motor development (folding, placing in appropriate location in drawer, pantry, or dishwasher). Tasks that aid in this skill are:

- Sorting laundry: pairing socks, folding washcloths, separating items into piles for each person
- Kitchen: set the table (silverware), load and unload the dishwasher (silverware and other items that belong in the lower cupboards), fold napkins
- Meal preparation: select items from pantry (by picture, color of jar, or food), put condiments on table (those in refrigerator that are kept on lower shelves)

2.) Compare/Contrast: Classification. Use every opportunity to identify categories for people, places, and things. Follow through on the activity in chapter 5 in which the children pick out what goes together or what does not belong among objects, pictures, or words. Example: Begin with "things that go," then things that "fly, go on the ground, or go on water," then things with motors. Continue with things that we ride in or on, and the activities get more and more detailed and complex. Use the various charts and tables that are displayed in this book to aid in this activity.

89

90   *Chapter 11*

3.) Fact/Opinion: In these next few activities, first identify words that designate a "fact" and others that designate an "opinion." The T-chart may be used for this purpose. Another format would be the diagram found in chapter 3. Children like to draw the oval and then all the lines outward. One diagram would be used for facts and another would be used for opinions. The child needs to participate as much as possible in the making of the charts or diagrams and the writing of words. In the case of young children, sometimes pictures may be used for the words.

4.) Fact/Opinion: Advertising. Using newspapers, magazines, and advertising flyers, cut out (fine motor skill for young children) the ads and place them in two piles, fact or opinion. Then discuss each pile separately and pick out what words proved the child's assessment. Follow the same procedure with the opinion pile of ads. For children who have not yet attained the reading skill level, put all the ads in one pile. Then read them to the children and allow them to decide whether it is factual or someone's opinion.

5.) Fact/Opinion: Advertising. Follow the same procedures as in #3, but this time, leave the ads intact and highlight the key words. Either highlight the facts in one color and opinions in another color or just highlight all the key words and then go back and discuss which are fact and which are opinions.

6.) Fact/Opinion: This is a research activity using math skills. If children are asked what the favorite lunch item is, their answer will probably reflect what their own favorite is. Teach them skills to prove their theory. First, select the child's opinion of the top four favorites for children: pizza, hamburgers (cheeseburgers), hot dogs, or spaghetti. Next, collect the data. This may be done in the following ways, using all or just one of the ideas:

- Ask the school cafeteria manager for the total number of each type of lunch that was purchased for one month. The manager keeps records, so it will not be a time-consuming task, and school personnel are receptive to helping the students in a research project. This information may be by grade level or total school.
- Ask relatives for the same information. The students in a sixth-grade class were asked to interview senior citizens and inquire as to what they believed was the greatest invention. One boy telephoned his grandmother long distance and asked her for her opinion. He was surprised when she answered, "my computer." He expected her to answer that the refrigerator or dishwasher or washing machine was by far the most important. He questioned her choice of response. She replied, "The computer brings the world right to my doorstep."
- Make a simple survey listing the four items and have the classmates or family rate them, 1 to 4, according to their preferences.

Investigating   91

Decide the form in which to display the data. Everyone has their own particular tastes, but this type of display shows what items are most popular. This may be in the form of a matrix or a graph. Forms for graphs—bar, line, circle/pie, or pictograph—are in some publishing software programs. These are examples of some types of graphs. Children need to know how to both create them and read them. This is a tested skill in the math section of standardized tests. Simply change the data for your own purpose.

7.) Fact/Opinion: Review a story, movie, or event. After experiencing any of the three, write a list of facts and opinions of the event. Use words or phrases; sentences are not necessary. The children might interview other folks who were there to obtain their version of the event. Facts can be proven. Example: Fact: the book was fifty pages long. Opinion: the book was exciting. This is also a lesson in vocabulary. Require the child to use a few different words for each description.

8.) Reality/Fantasy: This activity is for younger children. When selecting books, "read" the cover. Children learn to read pictures before they read words. Say to the child, "Tell me about the picture." Next, ask "Could this really happen?" Then discuss what the children think the story will be about and teach "fantasy" and "reality." This discussion also will help the children decide whether or not they think they might enjoy the story. If they are still undecided, use the rule of thumb to read the first two pages (this works for adults, too). If you are searching online, the book sites usually will have a page to view to help in the selection.

9.) Reality/Fantasy: At the time of each holiday, research the history of the custom and discuss whether it is reality or fantasy. Points to consider

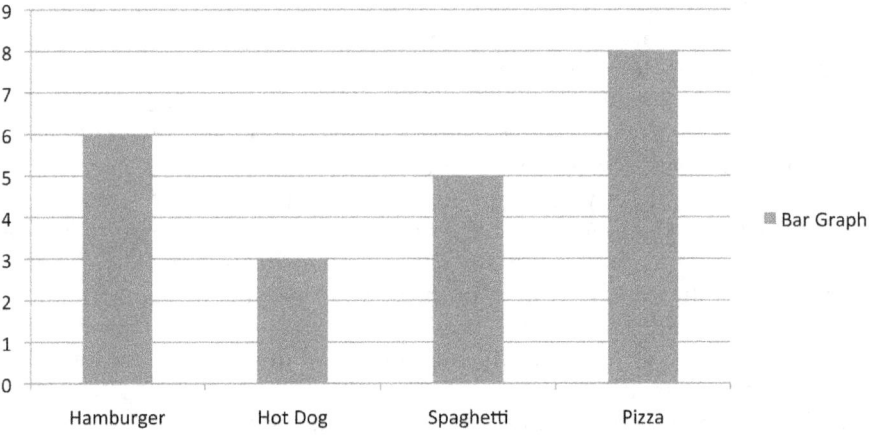

Figure 11.1. Bar Graph: Bar graphs show comparisons at a glance, in this case, pizza (8 people), hamburger (6), spaghetti (5), and hot dog (3). *Created by Guinevere Durham*

92 *Chapter 11*

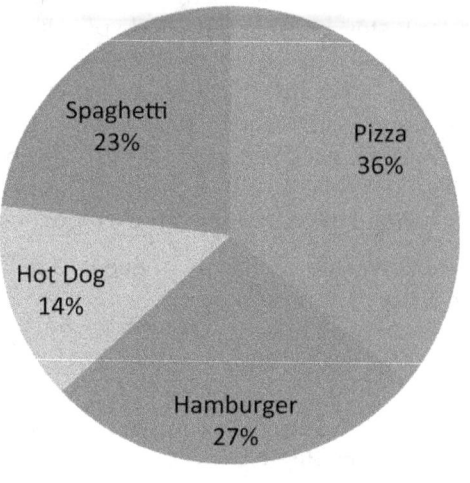

Figure 11.2.   Circle/Pie Graph: This type of graph shows the relationship of parts to the whole. *Created by Guinevere Durham*

are (1) when the custom originated, (2) where it originated, (3) has it changed over the years, (4) why it is celebrated, and, most important to the children, (5) how it relates to them. Even if the children don't believe in the concept or celebrate the particular holiday, expose the children to what it means. Then discuss why it is or is not celebrated in their home.

10.) Fact/Opinion and Compare/Contrast: This activity is a good follow-up to #9. The concept here is "Just because everyone else celebrates it or has it or wears it, doesn't mean we have to do the same." Start the discussion with the whys of the situation. When the children want the latest device in technology, designer jeans, or sneakers of a favorite athlete, do the research. Use the charts and activities to compare and contrast and decide whether the statements in the ads are facts or opinions. An issue that will be important in this case is budget. These two skills are not simply useful for evaluating stories, movies, or events only; they are used to evaluate issues in life.

11.) This last activity encompasses all of the investigative skills. There are times when the children's behavior is far more active than usual for them, or they may be "out of sorts" or "going through a phase." Some symptoms indicate a visit to a physician (temperature, aches or pains, vomiting). Consider those first. If all is well in those areas, consider this activity. The idea for this activity was presented in a parent-teacher meeting at an elementary school.

The PTA president had invited a local pediatrition to speak on ADHD (attention deficit hyperactivity disorder) and ADD (attention deficit disorder). The doctor spoke from both personal and professional experience. He grew up in a home with a sister who was diagnosed with ADHD and

Investigating   93

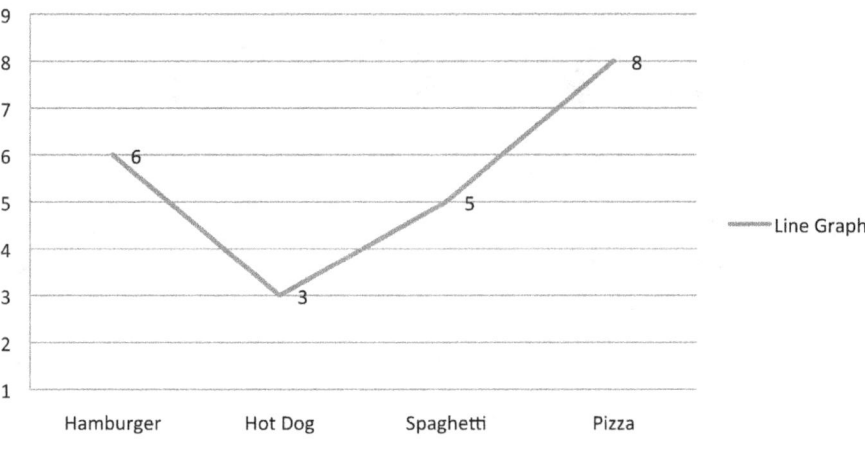

Figure 11.3.   Line Graph: A line graph shows a pattern of facts. *Created by Guinevere Durham*

in his profession, studied and researched the subject. He suggested that the parent keep a log of everything the children puts in their mouth for a week. In addition, the parent needed to document the daily behavior. Teachers would be agreeable to documenting the behavior at school.

The foods we eat today have many additives and preservatives that may affect the children adversely. Each child needs to be monitored individually, as each child reacts differently to the products. The list of contributing ingredients is endless; thus, when a change of behavior is documented, check which foods the particular child has eaten and read labels.

This activity is time-consuming, costs nothing, and will supply the parent with information significant to the children's health. Adults may keep the log for young children (with their input and participation), and middle and high school students will learn a lot from taking on the task themselves. In the few weeks that followed, several parents commented on how informative and helpful this activity was in their family. Some made it a family affair and kept the log for every member. The staff at the school all participated and found, to their surprise, some items to avoid.

94   Chapter 11

Hamburger

Hot Dog

Pizza

Spaghetti

Figure 11.4.   Pictograph: A pictograph uses pictures to show information. Children may be given a sticky-note and told to draw a picture of their favorite food. These are then put on a chart to form a graph as illustrated below. *Graph format created by Guinevere Durham; pictures of food created by Kyle Frinkley*

TWELVE

Experimenting

TECHNIQUES, STRATEGIES, AND ACTIVITIES

1.) A favorite activity for primary students is to make gelatin. First, depending on the reading level of the students, either a student or the teacher reads the directions (for auditory learners). A copy of the back of the package (for visual learners) was given to each student. The students highlighted the key words for the process. Someone always asked why the water had to be both hot and cold. The reply was, "Let's find out." Then the class was separated into five groups. Each group used a different procedure:

- Two cups of cold water is used.
- Two cups of hot water is used.
- One cup of hot water and one cup of ice cubes is used.
- One cup of hot water and a half cup each of cold water and ice cubes is used.
- One cup of hot water and one cup of cold water is used.

The students put the mixture in the refrigerator and checked it every hour throughout the day. They looked for the following: (1) did the crystals dissolve? (2) did it set? (3) how fast did it set?

The discussion that followed considered the "whys" of the finished product. The word "dissolve" was learned; to read it, to write it, and what it means. The depth of the discussion depended on the age level of the children.

2.) Baking projects are interesting and informative for experimentation with children. Some examples are:

- Bake bread with and without yeast.

95

96   *Chapter 12*

- Bake a cake from scratch (1) as per recipe, (2) without baking powder, (2) without baking soda, (4) without baking powder and baking soda.
- Follow the directions for a prepackaged cake or brownie mix and leave out the eggs.

For all of these projects, divide the basic batter into parts and then add the items to some but not the others. When baking is completed, check each part for texture, color, taste (this part will be a surprise), and size.

3.) The creation of a spider decoration for Halloween is a math activity. Have on display a model of the finished product, which consists of a six-inch round piece of black construction paper; four strips of black paper (one inch wide and the length of the paper, eleven inches) accordion-pleated and stapled in the bottom middle of the circular piece; and a piece of black yarn stapled on the top middle for hanging. Directions:

- Give the child a six-inch square of the black paper. For first- and second-graders, the next step takes quite a discussion, for they have to decide how to make a circle out of the square.
- Look at the "legs" and discuss how to make them pleated. The model has eight legs, but the child has only four strips of paper; thus, the concept of "half" again.
- Staple or glue the legs to the bottom and the yarn to the top and the spider is finished.
- Research "real" spiders and create a lesson on insects. A fun activity.

4.) Another favorite, especially for third-graders and up, is to write a message with "invisible ink." It is simple to do and requires four items: paper, lemon juice or lemons, a small paintbrush (use either end) or cotton swab, and a heat source (sunlight or lightbulb).These are the steps:

- Squeeze the lemons to obtain juice or use bottled lemon juice.
- Use the juice as the ink by dipping the paintbrush or swab in the liquid and writing the message. Let it dry.
- Hold the paper up to the light, at the window or up to a lightbulb. Be careful not to let the paper touch the lightbulb, as it may burn.
- The heat causes the writing to turn brown so the message may be read.
- Another way to read the message is to put salt on the drying ink. After a minute, shake off the salt and the message appears.
- Experiment with other juices (wine, orange juice, apple juice, and vinegar work well) to see what other substances work.

5.) When working on science projects, the vocabulary needs an explanation first. These are the basic terms and their meanings:

Experimenting 97

- Bibliography: A list of books, magazines, journals, encyclopedias, or websites used for background information. At least three different types are recommended.
- Conclusion: What the child learned from the data.
- Control: The part of the experiment that is not changed (as in following a recipe exactly) so that a comparison may be made.
- Data: All information from sources and that gathered from the experiment.
- Display: A visual exhibition of the procedure.
- Display Board: For schools, a three-sided cardboard upon which to put all the steps and information. Part of the experiment may be set on the table in front of the display board as verification (plants, cakes, etc.).
- Experiment: A process to discover something that is not known. Science experiments have a specific format to follow.
- Hypothesis: A guess the children make as to how they believe the experiment will turn out. Edison had the same hypotheses for each experiment; that is, there would be light.
- Log: A daily account of the steps performed and results witnessed.
- Research: The process of reading about the subject of the experiment.
- Materials: Everything the children need to conduct the experiment.
- Problem: What do the children want to find out or prove?
- Procedure: The steps to take in conducting the experiment.
- Results: What actually happened as a result of your work.
- Topic: The subject of the experiment.

6.) Scientific method: A typical school science project contains these steps:

- Pick the topic.
- State the problem.
- State the hypotheses.
- Gather all materials needed.
- Set up the procedure (plant the seeds, bake the bread or cakes, etc.).
- Keep a log. List procedures, make observations, and record data and results.
- State the conclusion.

7.) The "log" is the schematic of the whats, hows, and whys of the project and includes:

- Title page
- Table of contents
- Statement of the problem and the hypotheses
- List of materials
- Procedure
- All data

98   *Chapter 12*

- Results in the form of charts, graphs, tables, pictures, or lists
- Conclusions

The material may be in a pocket folder, a three-ring notebook, or a folder of computer-printed procedures. Place the document either on or in front of the display board. This should be written in the order of the steps taken in the process. The judges will consider the sequence of the steps and thoroughness of the information. Prepare it with great care.

8.) For many ideas of how to display the information of the children's projects, go to your search engine and type "examples of science fair display boards." To narrow the search, specify elementary, middle school, or high school. The selection to view is lengthy and very enlightening.

IV

The Keeping Fit

THIRTEEN

Proactive Steps for Physical Health

An ounce of prevention is worth a pound of cure. —Benjamin Franklin

This chapter is an "awareness" chapter. The information within provides caregivers of children the knowledge base with which to be proactive in protecting children's health.

The information is available from a multitude of sources. The rapid growth of technology resulted in a continuous quest for newer information. Graduate course work in early childhood education enumerated and explained the issues. From these answers came many more questions, which resulted in additional research. Some practical research came from teachers, coaches, and administrators in our school systems. The experiences of the parents, along with the knowledge of medical consultants, provide additional data. The consummate sources may be found on the Internet:

- American Academy of Ophthalmology
- American Academy of Pediatrics
- American Optometric Association
- American Physical Therapy Association
- American Academy of Orthopedic Surgeons

When the first personal computers were introduced to the public, they were primarily for adult use. What ensued was an "explosion of technical devices" of all shapes, sizes, and rational for usage. The use of these devices is no longer a luxury; they are a necessity. Children begin their education in this area as early as preschool.

However, accompanying this immense knowledge source are the detriments to the physical health and growth and development of children. Physicians in all genres offer proactive advice to caregivers for teaching

101

102   *Chapter 13*

the safe use of these products in the early childhood years. Five issues are
of importance for the children:

- Eyesight and eye stress
- Body position for health
- Repetitive stress injuries
- Social development as related to technology
- Increased pain in the shoulders, neck, back, and arms

EYESIGHT AND EYE STRESS

There are basic rules for protecting the eyes, no matter which device is
used (this also includes television). Children will need supervision until
the rules are understood and second nature to them.

- For every half hour, take a two-minute rest.
- Look head-on at the screen, without the need to tilt the head up or
  down.
- Check for glare or reflections of objects on the screen.
- Windows or light sources should not be directly visible when look-
  ing at the screen.
- A window either directly behind the monitor or directly behind the
  child may cause glare.
- Use blinds or drapes to filter the light.

The following are signs of concern to the proactive caregiver. These
signs may also carry over in the classroom or when doing homework.

- Blinking
- Tromboning (moving the head or body forward or back or side to
  side to get a clearer picture)
- Eye-focusing difficulty
- Head tilt (to one side or the other)
- Rubbing the eyes
- Redness of the eyes
- Dry eyes
- Headaches
- Struggle to finish a task or avoidance of the task (referring to
  schoolwork)

If the child is not working to potential in a classroom or other academic setting, review these issues. A vision exam may be needed from your
optometrist or ophthalmologist; this is your expert source.

A Georgia doctor, Rhonda Thompson, spends additional time discussing with several of her patients these "red flag" issues concerning eyesight in children. If diagnosed in childhood early, long-term problems
may be curtailed. She has also spoken to numerous college classes of

future nurses and teachers. Her suggestion to school PTAs and PTOs is to bring in a volunteer guest with this knowledge background to one of their meetings. This is a needed proactive strategy that will help children and parents. Since technology brings new issues to eye care in growing children, she stressed the awareness of caregivers in fostering their developing eyesight.

BODY POSITION FOR COMPUTERS

- Feet need to be flat on the floor, with a footstool if needed.
- Eyes are to look head-on to the screen, eighteen to twenty-eight inches from the screen. Prescription glasses can be made specifically for computer use.
- Forearms must be horizontal when using the keyboard. Use a mouse rather than the keyboard on the laptop. Arms cross over the body when using the laptop or notebook computer, causing pain.
- Every hour, stretch, take a walk, or change your activity.
- The backrest on the chair puts your body at a 90-degree angle.
- Do not use the armrests on the chair to slouch.

Signs of concern for the caregiver:

- Headaches
- Shoulder and neck pain
- Pain in the back or legs

REPETITIVE STRESS INJURIES

These injuries result from too much stress on a joint, caused by repetitive motion. It is common in athletes and those frequently using computers and handheld devices. A common malady is carpal tunnel syndrome, which is a swelling inside a "tunnel" formed by the bone and ligament in the wrist. To avoid some of the problems related to carpal tunnel syndrome:

- Remember to keep forearms level with the keyboard so you do not have to flex your wrists to type.
- Take periodic breaks to rest the hands, wrists, and fingers.

Signs for concern for the caregiver concerning wrist, fingers, and thumb issues are:

- Pain
- Numbness
- Tingling

104   *Chapter 13*

SOCIAL DEVELOPMENT

Excessive television viewing, texting, and playing computer games may interfere with and even displace reading and homework activities. Reading requires more thinking than these "fun" activities. Studies have shown that thinking results in healthy brain development.

Signs of concern for the caregiver:

- Sleeping problems
- Weight gain
- Poor performance in academics
- Personal interaction with friends is limited except in texting or e-mail or ceases to exist
- Physical activity diminishes, as in athletics, bike riding, or using playground equipment
- Activities involving imagination and creativity are curtailed
- Child is no longer talking with someone, only *to* someone

"Awareness" of these health, safety, and social issues allows the caregivers to be proactive in scheduling and prioritizing activities for a balanced lifestyle. Remember, awareness is the key. Don't let this information scare or overwhelm you. However, if the signs for concern develop into real symptoms, it is time to consult with a physician for a diagnosis and treatment.

The medical associations in addition to many universities have been researching these issues that have surfaced since the use of technology. A multitude of sources are available on the Internet that will give ideas and suggestions of activities and exercises for the children to help counterbalance the medical issues that arise with computer use. In the search engine, type in "tech overload causing kids physical problems" or "exercises for kids to prevent physical ailments resulting from technology use." The sources are endless and very informative. Check with the children's doctor as to what would be most effective for the children.

V
Aha!

FOURTEEN

Summary and Conclusion

This chapter is arranged in a format that guarantees that the important information has been emphasized and the subject matter has been presented in a format that is easily and quickly accessible. These are the highlights, but the details are in the chapters.

About the information:

- The five skills are not an entity unto themselves. They are compatible and interchangeable as needed.
- The child's style of learning (left-brained/right-brained) dictates the process in which the skill is taught and learned.
- Neither style of learning is "better"; they are simply different.
- The children's style of learning is inborn; thus, it is the right style for them.
- The activities, strategies, and techniques may be changed or expanded upon, or they may even set in motion an alternative, more appropriate activity for the children.
- What may work today may not work tomorrow.
- What may work for one child may not work for another child.
- The children need to be involved in the process and solution. The outcome is more readily acceptable when the children understand the "whys." Accepting it—yes. Liking it—maybe not.
- Teach to the child's strengths, using those strengths to compensate for or override the weaknesses.
- Allow other caregivers in the child's life to collaborate in the process.

This book is short and to the point and is jam-packed with useful information.

For the caregiver:

108   *Chapter 14*

- Read the book a chapter at a time, allowing for the processing of the information before going further.
- Highlight specifics that are proactive and need to be considered before the children experience the situation.
- Highlight (in a different color) other information that will be used in specific situations as they arise.
- Match the activities, strategies, and techniques to your child, your situation, and you.
- This book is not a "one-size-fits-all." As with any type of book, article, lecture, workshop, or conference, if you walk away from it with even a few ideas that will benefit you and your child, then the time, effort, and cost have been well spent.
- The five skills are fundamental to all children. "How," "how much," and "when" they are taught is unique for each child.
- Do not allow the information to overwhelm you or have you believing you have to do it all. Be practical, realistic, insightful, and ENJOY!

Breaking the Code: Definitions of Terms

Abstract learning: The ability to learn through the words, numbers, or symbols that represent real objects.

Auditory learner: A person whose primary way of learning is through "hearing" the information.

Bloom's Taxonomy: A classification of levels of intellectual behavior important in learning.

Caregiver: Parent, teacher, coach, counselor, grandparent, religious leader, or other relative or friend; that is, any person having a "say-so" stake in the education and upbringing of the child.

Cause/effect: A skill of comprehension: the cause is the actual event, the "why," and the effect is the result of what happened, the "what."

Child development areas:

1. Motor: Physical movement or agility
2. Adaptive: The body adjusting to the environment
3. Language: Words and sounds (phonics)
4. Personal/social: Relationships and reaction to others

Compare: Identification of similarities in two or more objects, events, places, or ideas.

Competency: The knowledge of or performance in a specific subject area.

Conclusion: What you learned from the results of the data and research

Concrete learning: Learning through the five senses: touch, sight, smell, taste, and hearing.

Context clues: Information from the sentence, paragraph, or story that help decode the unknown words or phrases.

Contrast: Identification of differences in two or more objects, events, places, or ideas.

Critical thinking: The skill of considering the facts: assessing, analyzing, and finally evaluating the information.

Early childhood: The years of birth through eight years of age, generally through the third-grade level in school.

110   *Breaking the Code: Definitions of Terms*

Experimenting: A process of discovery, either physical (as in a science lab or an invention) or academic (as in mathematics or other research) for something yet unknown.

Eye-hand coordination: The brain telling the hands and fingers to do what the eyes are seeing.

Eye orientation: The back-and-forth eye movement needed for observing and performing in the environment (for example, from marker/chalkboard to child's desk).

Fact: A truth or an actuality.

Fantasy: Make-believe, imagination, myth, a dream.

Fine motor skills: Skills involving the proficiency of the hands and fingers.

Hypothesis: A guess made as to the outcome of an investigation or experiment.

Inference: The skill of identifying what was implied but not stated.

Intelligence: The ability by which a person learns and understands through experience. (An intelligence test indicates how much the student is capable of learning.)

Intermediate level: Elementary school grades four through five or four through six, as defined by the school system.

Investigating: Searching in order to learn facts or information.

Key word(s): Words or phrases that "unlock" information.

Kinesthetic learner: A person who learns by physically "doing" the task.

Language arts: The curriculum areas of reading, spelling, English rules, and writing.

Large motor skills: Skills that involve the arms and legs (running, jumping, throwing, athletic feats, exercising).

Learning style: The way a person learns information, (left- or right-brained) or (auditorily, visually, or kinesthetically).

Left-brained: A learning style: analytical, logical, parts to the whole.

Literal: Interpreting statements or words according to their actual meaning; real; not going beyond the facts (sarcasm, irony, and some jokes are not understood by this person).

Logic: Sensible, rational thought or argument; a way of reasoning.

Main idea: The theme, topic, or what the story or event is all about.

Matrix: A chart used to compare two or more items, issues, or events.

Modality: A style of learning, visual, auditory, or kinesthetic.

Opinion: A belief, a judgment, or a feeling.

Predicting: Guessing; using past experience, education, or facts to predict what will happen in the future.

Prerequisite: A skill or class that needs to be accomplished before the next step (for example, addition and subtraction before multiplication or division).

Preschool level: The years before formal kindergarten.

Breaking the Code: Definitions of Terms   111

Primary level: Kindergarten through third grade.

Proactive: To consider possible scenarios and plan ahead the strategies or techniques to use as needed.

Problem solving: Finding an answer, a clue, a key, an explanation, or a clarification.

Reality: What can actually happen or what is true or factual.

Results: The collection of data or facts (the conclusion is the decision made from the results).

Right-brained: A learning style: global, random, creative, whole picture, then the parts.

Semiconcrete learning: Learning through pictures or symbols that represent real items.

Sequence: An order of succession, a continuity of progression, or a step-by-step process, each step necessary before the next step.

Strategies: The plan of action in a situation.

Summarizing: Identifying the main point of a story, situation, or event.

T-chart: A chart used to compare the pluses and minuses of one item or issue.

Techniques: How one carries out the plan of action.

Venn diagram: A diagram using overlapping circles to show relationships between people, objects, or issues.

Visual learner: A person whose primary method of learning is through sight.

Resources

CHAPTER 1

1.) Buzon, Tony. *Use Both Sides of Your Brain*. London, England: A Pluma Book (Penguin Group), 1991.

Tony Buzon has done extensive research on the working of the human brain. He is one of the world's leading authorities on learning techniques, and his book provides step-by-step exercises for discovering the powers of using the right side of the brain and learning to use the left side of the brain more effectively.

2.) Rose, Colin. 1987. Developed the Accelerated Learning reading program for schools.

3.) Marcon, Rebecca A. *Fourth-Grade Slump: The Cause and the Cure*, 1990–1993. Washington, DC, preschools project. Marcon is a developmental psychologist and associate professor of psychology at the University of North Florida in Jacksonville.

This project was begun in 1986–1987 in the District of Columbia Public Schools, Center for Systemic Educational Change. It was titled *Early Learning and Early Identification Follow-Up Study: Transition from the Early to the Later Childhood Grades.* The purpose was to ascertain "why so many bright, achieving children in the primary grades have difficulty making the transition to the upper elementary grades."

CHAPTER 2

1.) Hoffman, Eva. *Teaching Experience* magazine. Autumn 2003.

Eva Hoffman began her career in Poland and spent many years teaching and directing projects all over Europe to foster her ideas of *learning how to learn.* She was an independent educational consultant and co-founder/director of Learn How to Learn, Inspired Learning, and Eva Hoffman Education. She has conducted several workshops in Argentina, Austria, France, Holland, Indonesia, Italy, Ireland, Kenya, Poland, Spain, Sweden, and the United States. She has authored several books on the subject

114   *Resources*

CHAPTER 3

2.) Glaser, Edward M. *An Experiment in the Development of Critical Thinking.* Teachers College, Columbia University, 1941. Edward Glasser's fields were biotechnology and nutrition. He was the founder of Human Interaction Research Institute in 1961. It closed in 2014. He wrote and coauthored several books between 1948 and 1962. He received nine citations for his work.

CHAPTER 7

1.) Gesell, Arnold, Frances I. Ilg, and Louise Bates Ames. *The Child from Five to Ten.* New York: Harper & Row Publishers, revised 1977.

These authors studied, in great detail, child behavior and were instrumental in the operation of the original Yale Clinic of Child Development, which is now the Gesell Institute of Child Development. They were trained as examiners of the Gesell School Readiness Test. The training was followed by additional training for qualification as members of a cadre of teachers to train other classroom teachers in the philosophy of child behavior and as examiners of the test in a large school system.

To further research these topics, type any of the subject areas into your favorite search engine. There is a wealth of information from which to choose. Many sites offer activities, strategies, and lesson plans that are written for the specific age of your child.

- Logic
- Critical thinking
- Problem solving
- Investigating
- Experimenting
- Modalities
- Left-brain/right-brain
- How to learn

About the Author

Guinevere Durham, PhD, a retired educator of thirty years, writes from three perspectives: as an elementary principal, a classroom teacher, and a mother of six.

www.ingramcontent.com/pod-product-compliance
Lightning Source LLC
Chambersburg PA
CBHW070734230426
43665CB00016B/2240